gettyimages

1910s

gettyimages

1910s

Decades of the 20th Century
Dekaden des 20. Jahrhunderts
Décennies du XXᵉ siècle

Nick Yapp

KÖNEMANN

This edition ©Tandem Verlag GmbH
KÖNEMANN is a trademark and an imprint of Tandem Verlag GmbH
Photographs ©2001 Getty Images

This book was produced by Getty Images
Unique House, 21–31 Woodfield Road, London W9 2BA

For KÖNEMANN:	For Getty Images:
Managing editor: Sally Bald	Art director: Michael Rand
Project editors: Lucile Bas, Meike Hilbring	Design: B+B
Translation into German: Sebastian Wohlfeil	Picture editor: Ali Khoja
Translation into French: Francine Rey	Editor: Richard Collins
	Proof reader: Elisabeth Ihre
	Editorial assistance: Tom Worsley
	Special thanks: Tea McAleer

Typesetting by Roman Bold & Black, Cologne.

Printed in China

ISBN 3-8331-1078-3

10 9 8 7 6 5 4 3 2 1
X IX VIII VII VI V IV III II I

Frontispiece: Three and a half years into the war, Captain and newly-promoted
Mrs Dunville duck under an arch of Lewis guns as they leave the church after their
wedding in April 1918.

Frontispiz: April 1918: Als Captain Dunville und seine frisch gebackene Gemahlin
unter einem Ehrenspalier von Lewis-Gewehren nach der Trauung die Kirche
verlassen, herrscht schon dreieinhalb Jahre lang Krieg.

Frontispice : En avril 1918, après trois ans et demi de guerre, le capitaine Dunville et
sa jeune épouse passent sous une haie d'honneur de fusils Lewis. Ils viennent de
quitter l'église qui a célébré leur mariage.

Contents / Inhalt / Sommaire

Introduction

The decade from 1910 to 1919 witnessed the troubled teenage years of the 20th century. They were years of protest, aggression, disappointment, *angst* and bitter disillusion. The hopes that the new century had brought a decade earlier were mown down in a fusillade of wars, revolutions, strikes and armed insurrections culminating, between 1914 and 1918, in the mass slaughter of the First World War.

Blood stained much of the world – Mexico, Ireland, the Middle East, China, India, Africa, South America and, above all, Europe. Incompetent kings and bewildered statesmen were assassinated – an increasingly easy task with modern weapons. Democratic governments reeled under attacks from women and workers, for the dual spectres of militant suffragettes and organised labour were more than most governments could tolerate. In 1911 Britain was crippled by a series of strikes involving seamen, dockers, miners and railwaymen. At much the same time, the French Ministry of the Interior prepared its 'carnet B', a list of the trade unionists to be arrested in the event of war. A year later the German army was called out to deal with strikers in Hamburg and the Ruhr. On the eve of the First World War, Italy ground to a halt in the national strike of 'Red Week'.

Through it all shone the brilliance of human achievement. It was a decade that began with Stravinsky's *Firebird* and Bertrand Russell's *Principia Mathematica*, and ended with the foundation of the Bauhaus and the first visit to Europe of the Original Dixieland Jazz Band. Between these milestones Roland Garros flew across the Mediterranean, and Alcock and Brown crossed the Atlantic. Amundsen beat Scott to the South Pole. Marie Stopes published *Married Love*, and Gandhi led the Indian Independence Movement. Chaplin arrived at the Keystone Film Company in Hollywood, and D W Griffith produced *The Birth of a Nation*.

The last horse-drawn bus disappeared from the streets of London, and the first regular passenger flights between London and Paris were inaugurated. A bold aviator made the world's first parachute jump, and a bold editor published the first copy of *Pravda*. Doctor Harry Plotz discovered a typhus vaccine; Henry Ford set up the world's first assembly line.

For almost the last time, French, German, Italian and Spanish politicians deluded themselves that Europe was the cultural, industrial and financial hub of the world. The ancient order maintained its Ruritanian elegance and atavistic pomp and ceremony. But by 1919 the brave old continent was exhausted. Sooner or later the might of both the United States and the new Union of Soviet Socialist Republics would have to be recognised.

Einführung

Das Jahrzehnt von 1910 bis 1919 sah die aufgeregten Backfischjahre des 20. Jahrhunderts. Es waren Jahre des Protestes, der Aggression, der Enttäuschung, der Verängstigung und bitterer Desillusionierung. Die Hoffnungen, die das neue Jahrhundert im Jahrzehnt zuvor erweckt hatte, wurden dahingemäht in einem Sperrfeuer von Kriegen, Revolutionen, Streiks und bewaffneten Aufständen, die zwischen 1914 und 1918 in der Massenabschlachtung des Ersten Weltkrieges gipfelten.

Blutbefleckt stand ein großer Teil der Welt da – Mexiko, Irland, der Nahe Osten, China, Indien, Afrika, Südamerika und – vor allem – Europa. Unfähige Könige und verstörte Staatsmänner wurden ermordet – was mit modernen Waffen zunehmend leichter fiel. Demokratische Regierungen gerieten unter den Attacken von Frauen und von Arbeitern ins Wanken, denn die doppelte Bedrohung durch militante Suffragetten und eine organisierte Arbeiterschaft war mehr, als die meisten Staaten ertragen konnten. Im Jahre 1911 wurde Großbritannien durch eine Streikwelle gelähmt, an der Seeleute, Hafenarbeiter, Bergleute und Eisenbahner beteiligt waren. Ungefähr um dieselbe Zeit legte das französische Innenministerium sein „carnet B" an, eine Liste von Gewerkschaftlern, die im Kriegsfall zu inhaftieren waren. Ein Jahr später wurde deutsches Militär gegen Streikende in Hamburg und im Ruhrgebiet mobilgemacht. Am Vorabend des Ersten Weltkrieges kam ganz Italien im Generalstreik der „Roten Woche" praktisch zum Stillstand.

Hinter all dem leuchteten großartige menschliche Leistungen auf. Das Jahrzehnt begann mit Strawinskis *Feuervogel* und Bertrand Russells *Principia Mathematica* und endete mit der Gründung des Bauhauses und dem ersten Besuch der Original Dixieland Jazz Band in Europa. Im Zeitraum zwischen diesen Meilensteinen überflog Roland Garros das Mittelmeer und Alcock und Brown überquerten den Atlantik. Amundsen schlug

Scott im Wettlauf zum Südpol. Marie Stopes veröffentlichte *Married Love* und Gandhi führte die indische Unabhängigkeitsbewegung an. Chaplin fand sich bei der Keystone Film Company in Hollywood ein und D. W. Griffith produzierte *The Birth of a Nation*. Der letzte Pferdeomnibus verschwand aus den Straßen Londons und erste regelmäßige Passagierflüge zwischen London und Paris wurden eingeführt. Ein mutiger Flieger sprang zum allerersten Mal mit dem Fallschirm ab und ein mutiger Verleger publizierte das erste Exemplar der *Prawda*. Dr. Harry Plotz entdeckte den Impfstoff gegen Typhus; Henry Ford stellte das erste Fließband der Welt auf.

Beinahe zum letzten Mal konnten sich französische, deutsche, italienische und spanische Politiker vormachen, Europa sei der kulturelle, industrielle und finanzielle Nabel der Welt. Die alte Ordnung hielt an der Fiktion einer Bilderbuchmonarchie und an ihrem atavistischen zeremoniellen Prunk fest. Bis 1919 hatten sich die Kräfte des tapferen alten Kontinents allerdings erschöpft. Früher oder später würde man sowohl die Macht der Vereinigten Staaten als auch der Union der Sozialistischen Sowjetrepubliken anerkennen müssen.

Introduction

La décennie qui débuta en 1910 et s'acheva en 1919 fut le témoin des années troubles du XXᵉ siècle encore adolescent. Ce fut une période de contestation, de violence, de déception, d'angoisse existentielle et de désillusion amère. Les espoirs que le nouveau siècle avait suscités une décennie plus tôt furent anéantis par une succession de guerres, de révolutions, de grèves et d'insurrections armées qui culmina, de 1914 à 1918, avec le gigantesque massacre de la Première Guerre mondiale.

Le monde entier ou presque fut taché de sang – le Mexique, l'Irlande, le Moyen-Orient, la Chine, l'Inde, l'Afrique, l'Amérique du Sud et surtout l'Europe. Des rois incapables et des hommes d'État incrédules furent assassinés – une tâche que les armes modernes rendaient de plus en plus facile. Des gouvernements démocratiques furent ébranlés par les revendications de femmes et d'ouvriers car, pour la plupart de ces gouvernements, le double spectre des suffragettes militantes et des syndicats constituait une menace plus qu'intolérable. En 1911, la Grande-Bretagne fut paralysée par une série de grèves conduites par des marins, des dockers, des mineurs et des cheminots. Quasiment à la même époque, le ministre de l'Intérieur français rédigea son « carnet B » qui dressait la liste des syndicalistes à arrêter en cas de guerre. Un an plus tard, l'armée allemande fut appelée à la rescousse pour écraser les grévistes de Hambourg et de la Ruhr. À la veille de la Première Guerre mondiale, l'Italie fut immobilisée par un mouvement de grève nationale, la fameuse « semaine Rouge ».

Cette décennie fut aussi celle durant laquelle l'intelligence de l'homme et ses accomplissements rayonnèrent. Elle débuta avec l'*Oiseau de feu* de Stravinsky et les *Principia Mathematica* de Bertrand Russell et se termina avec la création du Bauhaus et la première tournée en Europe de l'Original Dixieland Jazz Band. Entre ces événements marquants, Roland Garros traversa la Méditerranée en avion tandis qu'Alcock et Brown réussissaient la traversée de l'Atlantique. Amundsen arriva au pôle Sud avant Scott. Marie Stopes publia *Married Love* et Gandhi dirigea le mouvement d'indépendance indien. Chaplin fit ses débuts chez Keystone Film Company à Hollywood et D. W. Griffith réalisa *Naissance d'une nation*. Le dernier bus tiré par des chevaux disparut des rues de Londres et les premiers vols réguliers de passagers entre Londres et Paris furent inaugurés. Un aviateur téméraire effectua le premier saut en parachute au monde pendant qu'un éditeur courageux publiait la première édition de la *Pravda*. Le Dr Harry Plotz découvrit le vaccin contre le typhus et Henry Ford inventa la première chaîne de montage au monde.

Pour la dernière fois ou presque, les politiciens français, allemands, italiens et espagnols entretinrent l'illusion que l'Europe était le centre culturel, industriel et financier du monde. L'ordre ancien maintenait l'illusion d'un royaume imaginaire dont les fastes et les pompes étaient ceux d'un autre temps. Mais, en 1919, le vieux continent était à bout. Tôt ou tard, la puissance des États-Unis et de la nouvelle Union des Républiques soviétiques socialistes devrait être reconnue.

1. Conflict
Konflikte
Les conflits

In the early days of Dr Sun Yat-sen's government in China, a crowd gathers to view the decapitated bodies of robbers. The old Manchu ways of summary justice remained.

In den frühen Tagen der Regierung Sun Yat-sens in China versammelt sich eine Menge um die enthaupteten Leichen von Räubern. Die Schnellverfahren der alten Mandschu-Justiz blieben erhalten.

Le régime de Sun Yat-sen en Chine ne fait que commencer et une foule s'est rassemblée pour regarder les corps décapités de voleurs. Les vieilles méthodes manchoues de justice sommaire subsistaient.

1. Conflict
Konflikte
Les conflits

The whole world lost its temper. For centuries the poor, hungry and oppressed masses had endured hardship and deprivation with the tolerance of despair. European powers had enslaved one third of the world and exploited as much again. Women had accepted the status of second-class citizens in even the most civilised of societies. Labour had kowtowed to bosses who ranged from the considerate to the cruel. The status quo had rarely been seriously challenged. Now came wars of independence, national strikes, protests by women. From all quarters there were strident demands for change and reform. There was a new spirit abroad. Worse, there was a new spirit at home.

Old empires tried to hit back, but most were unfit for the struggle. The Ottoman Empire reeled under attack by the Balkan League. The Chinese Empire disintegrated in the bloodbath of civil conflict. The Russian and Austro-Hungarian empires shrivelled and died. The British Empire somehow held on, though the cost of protecting and, at the same time, repressing its increasingly discontented colonies was beginning to prove too much.

The world was about to explode.

Die ganze Welt verlor die Fassung. Jahrhundertelang hatten die armen, hungrigen und unterdrückten Massen Härten und Entbehrung mit dem Mut der Verzweiflung ertragen. Die europäischen Mächte hatten ein Drittel der Welt versklavt und beuteten ein weiteres Drittel aus. Selbst in den zivilisiertesten Gesellschaften hatten Frauen den Status von Staatsbürgern zweiter Klasse hingenommen. Die Arbeiterschaft kuschte vor Bossen jeglicher Couleur, von den einsichtigen bis zu den skrupellosen. Der Status quo war selten ernsthaft in Frage gestellt worden. Jetzt kam es zu Unabhängigkeitskriegen, landesweiten Streiks, Protestaktionen von Frauen. Aus allen Lagern kamen lautstarke Rufe nach Veränderungen und Reformen. Ein neuer Geist wehte durch die Welt. Schlimmer noch, der neue Geist wehte auch vor der eigenen Haustür.

Die alten Reiche versuchten sich zu wehren, aber die meisten waren für den Kampf nicht gerüstet. Das Osmanische Reich wankte unter den Angriffen des Balkanbundes. Das kaiserliche China zerfiel im Blutbad des Bürgerkrieges. Das russische Zarenreich und die k. u. k. Monarchie Österreich-Ungarn welkten und starben. Das britische Empire hielt sich irgendwie, obwohl es sich abzeichnete, dass ihm die Kosten für die Erhaltung und gleichzeitige Unterdrückung seiner zunehmend unzufriedenen Kolonien langsam über den Kopf wuchsen.

Die Welt stand kurz vor der Explosion.

Le monde entier se mit en colère. Pendant des siècles, les masses pauvres, affamées et opprimées avaient enduré les épreuves et les privations avec la tolérance du désespoir. Les puissances européennes avaient réduit en esclavage un tiers de la planète et exploité un autre tiers. Les femmes avaient accepté le statut de citoyen de seconde classe, même au sein des sociétés les plus civilisées. Les ouvriers avaient fait la courbette devant leurs patrons. Jusque-là, le statu quo n'avait été que rarement défié. L'heure était maintenant aux guerres d'indépendance, aux grèves nationales et aux manifestations féministes. De toute part émergeaient de violentes revendications en faveur de changements et de réformes. Un nouvel état d'esprit était perceptible dans le monde. Pire, ce nouvel état d'esprit commençait à se faire sentir également chez soi.

Les vieux empires tentèrent une contre-attaque, mais la plupart d'entre eux furent incapables de résister. L'Empire ottoman vacilla sous le feu de l'entente balkanique. L'Empire chinois se désintégra dans un bain de sang causé par la guerre civile. Les Empires russe et austro-hongrois se consumèrent et moururent. L'Empire britannique résistait tant bien que mal, même si le coût engendré par la protection et la répression de ses colonies toujours plus mécontentes commençait à s'avérer trop élevé.

Le monde était sur le point d'exploser.

Winston Churchill – as Home Secretary (in top hat, on left of main group) – with armed police and members of the Scots Guards at the Sidney Street siege, Stepney, London, 3 January 1911. They were besieging a house of anarchists.

Winston Churchill – in seiner Eigenschaft als Innenminister (in der Hauptgruppe ganz links, mit Zylinder) –, bewaffnete Polizisten und Mitglieder der Schottischen Garde bei einer Polizeiaktion in der Sidney Street, Stepney, London, am 3. Januar 1911. Die Belagerung galt einem Anarchisten-Quartier.

Winston Churchill, alors ministre de l'Intérieur (en chapeau haut de forme, à gauche du groupe principal), des policiers et des membres de la Garde écossaise armés font le siège d'une maison occupée par des anarchistes à Sidney Street, dans le quartier de Stepney à Londres, le 3 janvier 1911.

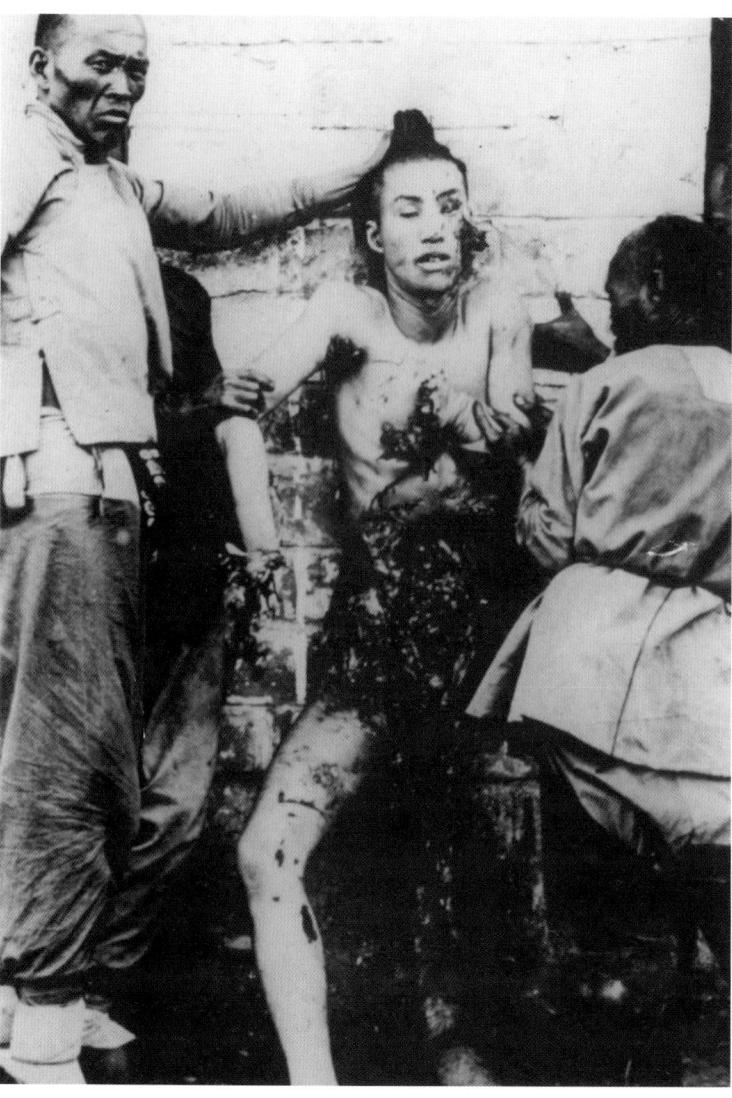

The victim of a bomb explosion (possibly his own bomb) is exhibited during the revolution in China, 1912.

Das Opfer einer Bombenexplosion (möglicherweise seiner eigenen) wird während der Revolution in China 1912 öffentlich vorgeführt.

La victime de l'explosion d'une bombe (peut-être sa propre bombe) est montrée au public durant la révolution en Chine, 1912.

Two foreigners gaze at a headless body in a city street in China, 1912. The revolution to overthrow Manchu rule boiled over into horrendous violence after the death of the Dowager Empress in 1908.

Auf der Straße einer chinesischen Stadt starren zwei Ausländer 1912 eine geköpfte Leiche an. Nach dem Tod der Witwe des Kaisers 1908 mündete die Revolution gegen das Mandschu-Regime in eine Welle fürchterlicher Gräueltaten.

Deux étrangers contemplent un corps sans tête dans une rue d'une ville chinoise, 1912. La révolution visant à renverser le régime manchou tomba dans une violence indescriptible après la mort de l'impératrice douairière en 1908.

The execution of a Chinese revolutionary, 1912. The term 'revolutionary' was widely construed to include anyone who opposed or criticised local, as well as national, authority. Scenes like this were common in town and country.

Exekution eines chinesischen Revolutionärs, 1912. Der Begriff „Revolutionär" wurde überaus großzügig ausgelegt und traf auf jeden zu, der sich in Wort oder Tat den örtlichen oder nationalen Behörden entgegenstellte. Szenen wie diese waren in Stadt und Land an der Tagesordnung.

Exécution d'un révolutionnaire chinois, en 1912. Le terme de « révolutionnaire » était assez vague pour inclure tous les opposants ou personnes critiques à l'égard des autorités locales et nationales. Des scènes comme celles-ci étaient courantes en ville et à la campagne.

By 1911 many supporters of the Old Order in China believed that a bloodbath was inevitable. This victim may have been pro- or anti-revolution. For many, it was simply a matter of being in the wrong place at the wrong time.

Bis 1911 waren viele Anhänger der alten Ordnung in China zu der Überzeugung gelangt, dass ein Blutbad unausweichlich sei. Dieses Opfer war vielleicht für, vielleicht gegen die Revolution. Viele waren einfach am falschen Ort zur falschen Zeit.

En 1911, pour beaucoup de partisans de l'ancien régime chinois, un bain de sang était devenu inévitable. Il est difficile de savoir si cette victime était pour ou contre la révolution. Souvent, cela tenait simplement au fait d'être au mauvais endroit au mauvais moment.

Unionists parade outside the City Hall, Belfast, 28 September 1912. They were queueing to sign Edward Carson's Solemn League and Covenant, which promised an armed struggle to fight against Home Rule for Ireland.

Mitglieder der Unionisten marschieren vor dem Belfaster Rathaus auf, 28. September 1912. Sie standen an, um Edward Carsons Solemn League and Covenant zu unterzeichnen – ein Dokument, das den bewaffneten Kampf gegen die Homerule, das Selbstbestimmungsrecht für Irland, in Aussicht stellte.

Les Unionistes manifestent devant le City Hall à Belfast, le 28 septembre 1912. Ils faisaient la queue pour signer le Covenant et la Ligue solennelle d'Edward Carson qui promettaient la lutte armée pour combattre le Home Rule en Irlande.

Sir Edward Carson in full flow, 1912. The introduction of the third Home Rule Bill to the House of Commons in 1912 infuriated the Ulster Unionists and led to the organisation by Carson of the Ulster Defence Volunteers.

Sir Edward Carson in Aktion, 1912. Die Vorlage des dritten Homerule-Gesetzes 1912 im Unterhaus erboste die Unionisten von Ulster und führte zur Organisation der Ulster Defence Volunteers durch Carson.

Sir Edward Carson en plein discours, en 1912. Le dépôt d'une troisième Home Rule Bill devant la chambre du Parlement en 1912 enflamma les Unionistes d'Ulster et conduisit Carson à créer la ligue des Ulster Defence Volunteers.

On the brink of war. Crowds gather for the funeral of one of the victims shot by the King's Own Scottish Borderers during what became known as the Bachelor's Walk massacre, Dublin, 29 July 1914.

Auf der Schwelle zum Krieg. Menschenmassen strömen zusammen, als eines der Opfer zu Grabe getragen wird, das beim später so genannten Massaker vom Bachelor's Walk von den King's Own Scottish Borderers erschossen wurde. Dublin, 29. Juli 1914.

Au bord de la guerre. Une immense foule s'est réunie pour l'enterrement d'une des victimes tuée par la Garde écossaise royale, tragédie qui fut ensuite appelée le Massacre de Bachelor's Walk, Dublin, le 29 juillet 1914.

A Scottish Borderer closes the door to the regiment's barracks after the massacre, 28 July 1914. Four civilians were killed and thirty-eight injured after soldiers failed to capture Irish Volunteers involved in gun-running at Howth.

Ein Mitglied der Scottish Borderers schließt nach dem Massaker das Tor zur Kaserne des Regiments, 28. Juli 1914. Bei dem fehlgeschlagenen Versuch, irische Freischärler bei einer Waffenschieberei in Howth gefangen zu nehmen, wurden vier Zivilisten getötet und 38 verletzt.

Un soldat de la Garde écossaise ferme la porte d'entrée aux baraquements du régiment après le massacre du 28 juillet 1914. Quatre civils furent tués et 38 blessés alors que les soldats tentaient en vain de capturer les «Volontaires irlandais» impliqués dans un trafic d'armes à Howth.

In a scene foreshadowing revolution on the streets of St Petersburg, police charge Irish strikers on the streets of Dublin, August 1913. One striker was killed and many injured.

In einer Szene, die den Ausbruch der Revolution in den Straßen St. Petersburgs vorwegnimmt, geht die Polizei auf den Straßen Dublins im August 1913 gegen irische Streikende vor. Ein Streikender kam ums Leben, viele wurden verletzt.

Ce cliché qui montre la police irlandaise tirant sur des grévistes dans une rue de Dublin anticipe une scène à Saint-Pétersbourg en pleine révolution, août 1913. Un gréviste fut tué et de nombreux autres furent blessés.

Three years after escaping execution in the aftermath of the Easter Rising, Eamon de Valera addresses a meeting in Los Angeles, December 1919. He was touring the United States as president of the Dail Eireann.

Drei Jahre nachdem er seiner Hinrichtung in der Folge des Osteraufstandes entgangen ist, spricht Eamon de Valera im Dezember 1919 vor einer Versammlung in Los Angeles. Er war auf einer Vortragsreise durch die Vereinigten Staaten als Präsident des irischen Parlaments.

Trois ans après avoir échappé à l'exécution suite à l'insurrection de Pâques, Eamon de Valera tient un meeting à Los Angeles, décembre 1919. Il était président du Dail Eireann, Chambre basse du Parlement irlandais.

The General Post Office, Sackville Street, Dublin, April 1916. It was here that the proclamation of the Irish Republic began the Easter Rising.

Die Hauptpost in der Sackville Street von Dublin im April 1916. Die Ausrufung der Republik Irland an dieser Stelle löste den Osteraufstand aus.

La poste centrale de Sackville Street à Dublin, avril 1916. Ce fut là que la proclamation de la République irlandaise déclencha l'insurrection de Pâques.

British troops in action near the Dublin quays during the Easter Rising, April 1916. One hundred British soldiers and 450 Irish fighters were killed.

Britische Truppen im Kampf in der Nähe der Kais von Dublin während des Osteraufstandes, April 1916. Hundert britische Soldaten und 450 irische Kämpfer wurden getötet.

Soldats britanniques à l'œuvre près des quais de Dublin durant l'insurrection de Pâques, avril 1916. Cent soldats britanniques et 450 combattants irlandais furent tués.

The charred shell of the General Post Office, Dublin, Easter 1916.
It was the focal point of the fighting in what many regard as the first
modern rising against colonial rule.

Die verkohlte Ruine der Hauptpost in Dublin, Ostern 1916. Hier lag
der Brennpunkt in einem Kampf, den viele als erstes modernes Beispiel
für die Auflehnung gegen die Kolonialherrschaft ansehen.

La voûte calcinée de la poste centrale de Dublin, Pâques 1916. Ce fut
là que convergèrent les combats considérés, par beaucoup, comme le
premier soulèvement moderne contre l'autorité coloniale.

Children in a poor area of Dublin collect firewood from the piles of rubble created by fighting during the Easter Rising. In general, the population of Dublin responded to the Rising with determined indifference.

Kinder in einem Armenviertel von Dublin sammeln Feuerholz aus den Trümmern, die die Kämpfer während des Osteraufstandes verursacht haben. Die Bevölkerung Dublins reagierte auf den Aufstand im Allgemeinen mit hartnäckigem Gleichmut.

Des enfants d'un quartier pauvre de Dublin ramassent du bois pour le feu parmi les ruines nées des combats menés pendant l'insurrection de Pâques. En général, la population de Dublin vécut l'insurrection dans une indifférence obstinée.

British muscles, 1919. The sign reads 'It is absolutely forbidden to cross this border into Afghan territory'. The British were there to prop up the failing White Russian cause after the Revolution of 1917.

Britisches Muskelspiel, 1919. Das Schild verkündet: „Das Überschreiten dieser Grenze zum afghanischen Territorium ist strengstens untersagt." Die Briten waren präsent, um den nach der Revolution von 1917 sinkenden Stern der russischen „Weißen" zu stützen.

Force britannique, 1919. Le panneau dit « Il est strictement défendu de traverser cette frontière et de pénétrer sur le territoire afghan ». Les Britanniques étaient là pour soutenir la cause vacillante des Russes blancs après la révolution de 1917.

Afghanistan muzzles, 1910. A group of tribesmen pose for the camera somewhere near the Khyber Pass. At the time, the area was unusually and disconcertingly quiet.

Afghanische Kriegspose, 1910. Afghanische Stammesangehörige bringen irgendwo in der Nähe des Khyber-Passes ihre Vorderlader in Anschlag. Damals herrschte in diesem Gebiet eine ungewohnte und beunruhigende Stille.

Fusils afghans, 1910. Des membres d'une tribu posent pour la caméra quelque part près du col de Khyber. À cette époque, la région était calme, ce qui était inhabituel et déroutant.

Members of General Francisco 'Pancho' Villa's rebel army enter the city of Sinaltua shortly after its capture during the Mexican Revolutionary War, November 1913. The war lasted until the 1920s.

Krieger der Rebellenarmee von General Francisco „Pancho" Villa strömen in die Stadt Sinaltua, kurz nachdem sie im mexikanischen Revolutionskrieg eingenommen worden ist, November 1913. Der Krieg dauerte bis in die zwanziger Jahre.

Des membres de l'armée rebelle du Général Francisco « Pancho » Villa pénètrent dans la ville de Sinaltua durant la guerre révolutionnaire mexicaine, en novembre 1913. La guerre dura jusque dans les années vingt.

Casualties of war lie on the streets of Mexico City. After the capture of Juárez in November 1913, Villa led his men on to the capital to take on the army of General Huerta, the *de facto* ruler of Mexico.

Kriegsopfer auf den Straßen von Mexico City. Nach der Einnahme von Juárez im November 1913 führte Villa seine Truppen in die Hauptstadt, um der Armee von General Huerta, dem eigentlichen Machthaber über Mexiko, entgegenzutreten.

Des victimes de la guerre gisent dans les rues de Mexico. Après la prise de Juárez en novembre 1913, Villa et ses hommes marchèrent sur la capitale pour se confronter à l'armée du Général Huerta, le chef d'État de facto du Mexique.

Emiliano Zapata,
leader of the rebels
in southern Mexico,
1915. Zapata was
part brigand, part
general.

Emiliano Zapata,
Anführer der
Aufständischen im
Süden Mexikos,
1915. Zapata war
teils Straßenräuber,
teils General.

Emiliano Zapata,
le chef des rebelles
du sud du Mexique,
1915. Zapata
était mi-brigand,
mi-général.

In the early days of the war, Pancho Villa leads a section of the rebel army, January 1911. Villa's fugitive life began at the age of 16 and ended twenty-nine years later in his death in a revenge killing.

Im Januar 1911, zu Beginn des Krieges, führt Pancho Villa eine Abteilung der aufständischen Armee an. Villas Leben im Untergrund begann im Alter von 16 Jahren und endete 29 Jahre später mit seinem gewaltsamen Tod in einem Racheakt.

Au début de la guerre, Pancho Villa fut en charge d'une section de l'armée rebelle, janvier 1911. La vie du fugitif Villa commença à 16 ans et s'acheva 29 ans plus tard quand il fut tué en représailles dans un attentat.

The suffragette Emily Davison is killed as she throws herself under the King's horse at the Epsom Derby, 4 June 1913.

Die Suffragette Emily Davison kommt ums Leben, als sie sich am 4. Juni 1913 beim Epsom Derby vor die Hufe eines Pferdes des Königs wirft.

La suffragette Emily Davison mourut en se jetant sous le cheval du roi à l'occasion du Derby d'Epsom, 4 juin 1913.

A militant suffragette is arrested during a day of disturbance in central London, 21 May 1914.

Eine militante Suffragette wird an einem Tag stürmischer Proteste im Zentrum Londons verhaftet, 21. Mai 1914.

Une suffragette militante est arrêtée lors d'une journée de protestation dans le centre de Londres, 21 mai 1914.

On the same day, the burly arms of the law remove Emmeline Pankhurst from the vicinity of Buckingham Palace. As active co-founder of the Women's Social and Political Union, she was used to being arrested.

Am selben Tag entfernen die starken Arme des Gesetzes Emmeline Pankhurst aus der Umgebung des Buckingham Palace. Als aktive Mitbegründerin der Women's Social and Political Union war sie an Festnahmen gewöhnt.

Le même jour, les gros bras de la police en civil emmènent Emmeline Pankhurst loin du Palais de Buckingham. Cofondatrice de l'Union sociale et politique des femmes, elle avait l'habitude d'être arrêtée.

A group of Austrians demonstrate for women's rights in Vienna,
19 March 1911. The slogan on the placard reads: 'Equal duties, equal
rights'. Austrian women were enfranchised in 1918.

Österreicherinnen demonstrieren am 19. März 1911 unter dem
Slogan „Gleiche Pflichten, gleiche Rechte" in Wien für die Gleich-
berechtigung. Die Österreicherinnen erhielten das Wahlrecht 1918.

Un groupe d'Autrichiennes manifestent en faveur des droits de la
femme à Vienne, 19 mars 1911. Le slogan des affiches dit : « devoirs
égaux, droits égaux ». Les Autrichiennes furent « affranchies » en 1918.

Members of the National American Woman Suffrage Association parade in New York, 3 May 1913. Their persistence paid off in August 1920 with the ratification of the Nineteenth Amendment, giving American women the franchise on an equal basis with men. Thereafter the NAWSA ceased to exist.

Eine Demonstration der Frauenrechtlerinnen-Vereinigung National American Women Suffrage Association in New York am 3. Mai 1913. Die Beharrlichkeit zahlte sich aus: Im August 1920 erhielten die amerikanischen Frauen durch die Ratifizierung des 19. Verfassungsgrundsatzes das gleiche Wahlrecht wie die Männer.

Des membres du National American Woman Suffrage Association défilent à New York le 3 mai 1913. La persévérance dont elles firent preuve porta ses fruits en août 1920 avec la ratification du 19ᵉ amendement qui accorda aux Américaines le droit de vote. Après cette victoire, le NAWSA cessa d'exister.

Female fervour. An impassioned and impromptu speech by an American suffragette in a New York street, 1912.

Mitreißende Weiblichkeit. Die leidenschaftliche improvisierte Ansprache einer amerikanischen Suffragette 1912 auf den Straßen New Yorks.

Ferveur féminine. Une suffragette américaine délivre un discours passionné et improvisé dans une rue de New York, en 1912.

Male mockery. A group of men destroy a banner taken from a suffragette picket line outside the White House, Washington DC, 1912. There were many men who objected to women smoking and drinking, let alone voting.

Spottende Männlichkeit. Eine Männergruppe zerstört ein Transparent, das sie von einem Streikposten der Suffragetten vor dem Weißen Haus in Washington, D. C., 1912 erobert hat. Es gab viele Männer, die etwas dagegen hatten, dass Frauen rauchten oder tranken, geschweige denn wählten.

Moquerie masculine. Ces hommes détruisent une bannière arrachée à un piquet de grève de suffragettes tenu devant la Maison-Blanche à Washington DC, 1912. Nombreux étaient les hommes qui n'acceptaient pas que les femmes boivent et fument et, pire encore, qu'elles votent.

Miners in South Wales lubricate their dusty throats with pints of bitter and discuss the start of a major strike, 27 February 1912. Within five days, over a million of their colleagues had withdrawn their labour.

Bergarbeiter in Südwales befeuchten ihre staubigen Kehlen mit einem Pint Bier und besprechen den Beginn eines Großstreiks, 27. Februar 1912. Binnen fünf Tagen hatten mehr als eine Million ihrer Kollegen die Arbeit verweigert.

Des mineurs du sud du Pays de Galles étanchent leur soif avec une pinte de bière et discutent le lancement d'une grande grève, 27 février 1912. Cinq jours plus tard, plus d'un million de leurs collègues cessaient le travail.

A couple of hundred miles away, women mine workers stage a sit-down protest on a pile of coal at a mine near Wigan, Lancashire. Three weeks later, the British Government granted coal workers a minimum wage.

Ein paar 100 Meilen davon entfernt führen Bergarbeiterinnen einen Sitzstreik auf einer Kohlenhalde bei einer Mine in der Nähe von Wigan in Lancashire durch. Drei Wochen später garantierte die britische Regierung Bergarbeitern einen Mindestlohn.

À quelques centaines de kilomètres de là, des employées d'une mine près de Wigan (Lancashire) improvisent une grève sur le tas, assises sur un monticule de charbon. Trois semaines plus tard, le gouvernement britannique accordait un salaire minimum aux mineurs.

In October 1912, Bulgaria, prime mover of the Balkan League, declared war on the Ottoman Empire. Here a Bulgarian field gun is moved into position during the siege of Adrianople, August 1913.

Im Oktober 1912 erklärte Bulgarien, treibende Kraft des Balkanbundes, dem Osmanischen Reich den Krieg. Hier wird ein bulgarisches Feldgeschütz bei der Belagerung von Adrianopel (Edirne) im August 1913 in Stellung gebracht.

En octobre 1912, la Bulgarie, initiateur de l'entente des Balkans, déclara la guerre à l'Empire ottoman. Ici, un canon bulgare est mis en position de tir durant le siège d'Adrianople, août 1913.

Soldiers remove their dead comrades from the battlefield of Adrianople,
October 1913. The war was staggering towards its end, leaving a few
months of uneasy peace before the tragedy of Sarajevo.

Soldaten bergen im Oktober 1913 ihre gefallenen Kameraden auf dem
Schlachtfeld von Adrianopel. Der Krieg schleppte sich seinem Ende
entgegen; es blieben noch einige Monate eines unruhigen Friedens bis
zur Katastrophe von Sarajewo.

Des soldats évacuent leurs camarades tués sur le champ de bataille
d'Adrianople, octobre 1913. La guerre tirait à sa fin pour faire place à
quelques mois de paix incertaine avant la tragédie de Sarajevo.

Archduke Franz Ferdinand of Austria and the Duchess Sophia
prepare to leave Sarajevo ahead of schedule on the fateful afternoon
of 28 June 1914. An attempt had already been made on their lives.

Erzherzog Franz Ferdinand von Österreich und Herzogin Sophia
schicken sich an, Sarajewo an jenem verhängnisvollen Nachmittag
des 28. Juni 1914 vorzeitig zu verlassen. Es war bereits ein Anschlag
auf sie verübt worden.

L'archiduc François-Ferdinand d'Autriche et la duchesse Sophie
quittent Sarajevo plus tôt que prévu en ce fatidique après-midi
du 28 juin 1914. Un attentat visant à mettre fin à leurs jours avait
déjà eu lieu.

The royal cavalcade sets off for the railway station in Sarajevo. Moments later it took a wrong turning, stopped, and Gavrilo Princip struck.

Die Kolonne des Thronfolgers macht sich auf den Weg zum Bahnhof in Sarajewo. Nur Augenblicke später bog sie falsch ab, hielt an, und Gavrilo Princip schlug zu.

Départ de la cavalerie royale pour la gare de Sarajevo. Quelques instants plus tard, elle s'engagea dans une rue adjacente, s'arrêta et Gavrilo Princip tira.

Nedeljko Cabrinovic, one of Princip's fellow conspirators, is hustled away by police after his failed attempt at assassinating the Archduke. Princip's successful attempt was made a couple of hours later.

Nedeljko Cabrinovic, einer von Princips Mitverschwörern, wird nach seinem fehlgeschlagenen Attentat auf den Erzherzog von Polizeikräften abgedrängt. Princips erfolgreicher Versuch erfolgte ein paar Stunden später.

Nedeljko Cabrinovic, un des complices de Princip, est emmené par la police après sa tentative d'assassinat contre l'archiduc. Quelques heures plus tard, Princip réussissait son coup.

The bloodstained tunic of the Archduke is placed on display. The spark was about to set the world ablaze.

Der blutbefleckte Rock des Erzherzogs wird ausgestellt. Der Funke sollte die Welt in Flammen setzen.

La tunique de l'archiduc tachée de sang est montrée au public. Ce fut l'étincelle qui mit le monde en feu.

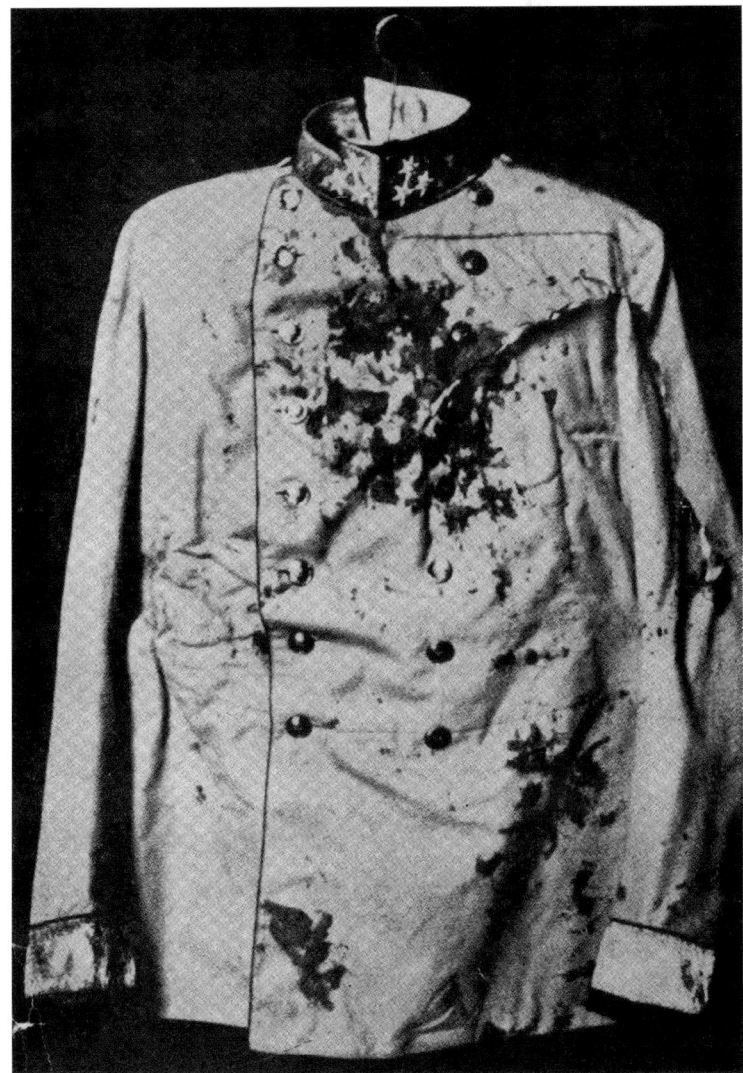

2. The Western Front
Die Westfront
Le front Ouest

French soldiers on the battlefield of Verdun, August 1917. For months the fortifications here were the flash point of the Western Front, a deadly test of strength between German and French armies.

Französische Soldaten auf dem Schlachtfeld von Verdun im August 1917. Monatelang waren die dortigen Befestigungen der Brennpunkt der Westfront, ein mörderisches Kräftemessen zwischen der deutschen und der französischen Armee.

Soldats français sur le champ de bataille de Verdun, août 1917. Pendant des mois, les forts constituèrent le centre névralgique du front Ouest, une épreuve de force mortelle pour les armées française et allemande.

2. The Western Front
Die Westfront
Le front Ouest

It was all going to be over by Christmas. Everyone said so – the French commanders, the Russian commanders, the British and German commanders. The Kaiser promised his troops, as they prepared to leave Berlin in August 1914, that they would be back 'before the leaves fall from the trees'.

But the war on the Western Front dragged on for 1,559 days, creating seas of mud and fields of slaughter from the Channel to the Swiss border. Men choked to death on poison gas, drowned in flooded shell holes, bled to death from shell and bullet wounds. The sacrifice made by the young and innocent at Ypres, Verdun, the Marne, the Somme, Passchendaele, Cambrai, Arras, Vimy Ridge and a hundred more killing fields was on an unprecedented scale.

Governments, profiteers, churchmen and generals demanded that they fight on. The dreadful doctrine of attrition was invoked to justify the tactics of slaughter: we have more men than the enemy, therefore the sooner all combatants are killed, the sooner we shall emerge as victors.

The grotesque parade marched on.

Bis Weihnachten sollte alles vorüber sein. Jeder sagte das – die französischen Befehlshaber, die russischen Befehlshaber, die britischen und die deutschen Befehlshaber. Der Kaiser versprach seinen Truppen, die im August 1914 aus Berlin ausrückten, sie würden heimkehren, „bevor die Blätter von den Bäumen fallen".

Aber der Krieg an der Westfront zog sich über 1559 Tage hin, in einem Meer von Morast und mit immer neuen Schlachtfeldern zwischen Ärmelkanal und Schweizer Grenze. Männer erstickten an Giftgas, ertranken in gefluteten Bombentrichtern, verbluteten an

Verletzungen durch Granaten und Kugeln. Die Opfer der Jungen und Unschuldigen in Ypern, Verdun, Passchendaele, Cambrai, Arras, an der Marne, der Somme, auf den Höhen von Vimy und auf hunderten weiteren Schlachtfeldern nahm Ausmaße an, die noch nie da gewesen waren.

Regierungen, Profiteure, Männer der Kirche und Generäle verlangten, dass weitergekämpft werde. Die schreckliche Doktrin des Zermürbungskrieges wurde heraufbeschworen, um die Strategie des Gemetzels zu rechtfertigen: Wir haben mehr Soldaten als der Feind, je mehr sich also gegenseitig umbringen, desto eher werden wir den Sieg erringen.

Die groteske Parade nahm ihren Lauf.

Tout serait terminé à Noël. C'était ce qu'ils disaient tous, qu'ils soient des généraux français, russes, britanniques ou allemands. Le « Kaiser » promit à ses troupes, qui s'apprêtaient à quitter Berlin en août 1914, qu'elles seraient de retour « avant que les feuilles des arbres ne tombent ».

Mais la guerre sur le front Ouest dura 1559 jours, engendrant des mers de boue et des champs de massacre qui s'étendirent de la Manche à la frontière suisse. Les hommes moururent asphyxiés par les gaz de combat, noyés dans des trous d'obus inondés, saignés à mort par des blessures d'obus et de balles. Le sacrifice d'hommes jeunes et innocents sur les champs de la mort d'Ypres, de Verdun, de la Marne, de la Somme, de Passchendaele, de Cambrai, d'Arras, de Vimy Ridge et des centaines d'autres fut sans précédent.

Gouvernements, profiteurs, hommes d'église, généraux, tous exigeaient qu'ils poursuivent la bataille. L'épouvantable doctrine de la guerre d'usure fut avancée pour justifier la tactique du massacre, qui se résumait en ces termes : « Nous avons plus d'hommes que l'ennemi, donc plus vite nous aurons tué les soldats ennemis, plus vite nous sortirons vainqueurs ».

Le macabre cortège poursuivit sa marche au combat.

Triumphant expectations. The declaration of war is read out in Berlin, August 1914.
'Let your hearts beat for God,' exhorted the Kaiser, 'and your fists on the enemy!'
In a surge of patriotism, men leapt at the chance to die.

In Erwartung des Triumphs. In Berlin wird im August 1914 die Kriegserklärung ver-
lesen. „Mögen eure Herzen für Gott schlagen", rief der Kaiser aus, „und eure Fäuste
den Feind!" In einer Aufwallung von Patriotismus rissen sich junge Männer um die
Chance zu sterben.

Espoirs de triomphe. La déclaration de guerre est lue en public à Berlin, août 1914.
« Que vos cœurs battent pour Dieu », exhorta l'Empereur, « et que vos poings battent
l'ennemi ! ». Emportés par une vague de patriotisme, les hommes sautèrent sur
l'occasion de mourir pour la patrie.

Cheering crowds greet Britain's declaration of war on Germany in
Trafalgar Square, London, 4 August 1914. Within a month, 17 million
men across Europe were engaged in fighting.

Jubelnde Massen begrüßen die Kriegserklärung Großbritanniens an
Deutschland am 4. August 1914 auf dem Trafalgar Square in London.
Binnen eines Monats waren 17 Millionen Männer in ganz Europa an
den Kampfhandlungen beteiligt.

Une foule enthousiaste salue la déclaration de guerre de la Grande-
Bretagne à l'Allemagne à Trafalgar Square (Londres), 4 août 1914.
En l'espace d'un mois, 17 millions d'hommes à travers toute l'Europe
furent engagés dans la bataille.

Recruiting posters in Fleet Street, London, 1915. The message at the top reads: 'If you are a whiteman prove your colour and courage now'.

Rekrutierungsplakate in der Londoner Fleet Street, 1915. Die Botschaft oben lautet: „Wenn Sie ein Weißer sind, dann beweisen Sie jetzt Ihre Farbe und Ihren Mut".

Affiches d'enrôlement à Fleet Street, à Londres, 1915. Le message en haut à droite dit : « Si vous êtes un homme blanc, c'est le moment de prouver votre couleur et votre courage ».

Would-be soldiers take the King's Shilling and the oath of allegiance at a recruiting office in Shepherd's Bush, London, December 1914. They came in all ages and from all classes.

Wehrwillige nehmen in einem Rekrutierungsbüro in Shepherd's Bush, London, im Dezember 1914 den Shilling des Königs entgegen und leisten den Treueeid. Sie kamen aus allen Altersgruppen und Schichten.

Après avoir reçu leur shilling, donné en échange de leur enrôlement, ces futurs soldats prêtent allégeance dans un bureau de conscription à Shepherd's Bush (Londres), décembre 1914. Les hommes qui s'y présentaient étaient issus de toutes les classes sociales et tranches d'âge.

Newly-kitted-out recruits line up for inspection in Bermondsey, London, 1915. Men such as these formed the backbone of Kitchener's New Armies. Within months they would be in the front line.

Frisch eingekleidete Rekruten lassen sich begutachten, Bermondsey, London, 1915. Männer wie diese bildeten das Rückgrat von Kitchener's New Armies. Nur Monate später standen sie an der Front.

Des recrues fraîchement équipées en rang pour une inspection à Bermondsey (Londres), 1915. Ces hommes-là constituaient l'épine dorsale des Nouvelles Armées de Kitchener. Dans quelques mois, ils seraient sur le front.

Two recruits receive their medical examination at Marylebone Grammar School, London, 1914. They were almost certainly among the first, for the school would have been requisitioned by the military for the summer holidays only.

Zwei Rekruten werden in der Oberschule von Marylebone in London 1914 auf ihre Tauglichkeit untersucht. Sie gehörten mit ziemlicher Sicherheit zu den Ersten, da die Schule vom Militär wohl nur in den Sommerferien beschlagnahmt wurde.

Deux recrues subissent un examen médical au lycée de Marylebone (Londres), 1914. Ils faisaient très certainement partie des premiers conscrits car l'armée n'aurait pas pu réquisitionner une école au-delà des vacances d'été.

Watched by anxious crowds, German troops march through the Place Rogier, Brussels, 20 August 1914. It had taken just over two weeks to reach the Belgian capital. The photograph was published in English and French newspapers.

Unter den Blicken ängstlicher Massen marschieren deutsche Truppen über den Place Rogier in Brüssel, 20. August 1914. Sie hatten nur gut zwei Wochen gebraucht, um die belgische Hauptstadt zu erreichen. Die Fotografie wurde in englischen und französischen Zeitungen veröffentlicht.

Sous le regard anxieux de la foule, les troupes allemandes défilent sur la place Rogier à Bruxelles, le 20 août 1914. Il ne leur avait fallu que deux semaines pour atteindre la capitale belge. Ce cliché fut publié dans les journaux français et anglais.

French reservists set out for army headquarters at the beginning of the
First World War, August 1914. In 1913 the French Government had
increased the period of compulsory military service to three years.

Französische Reservisten machen sich zu Beginn des Ersten Weltkrieges im August 1914 auf den Weg zu den Armeestützpunkten.
Im Jahre 1913 hatte die französische Regierung die Wehrpflicht auf
drei Jahre ausgedehnt.

Des réservistes français en route pour les quartiers généraux de
l'armée au début de la Première Guerre mondiale, août 1914.
En 1913, le gouvernement français allongea la durée du service
militaire obligatoire à trois ans.

'Goodbye, goodbye… wipe that tear, baby dear, from your eye…' – a British
soldier bids farewell to a loved one at Victoria Station, London, December 1914.
It was a scene that became tragically commonplace.

„Adieu, mein Schatz, adieu … und keine Tränen mehr …" – ein britischer Soldat
sagt seiner Liebsten Lebewohl, Dezember 1914 in der Victoria Station, London.
Eine Szene, die auf geradezu tragische Weise alltäglich wurde.

« Adieu, adieu … essuie cette larme, mon petit cœur, qui coule sur ta joue … ».
Un soldat britannique faisant ses adieux à sa fiancée en gare de Victoria (Londres),
décembre 1914. Cette scène devint tristement banale.

Families meet, place flowers on the helmets of their heroes, and part, as young German soldiers leave for the Front, 1914.

Familien versammeln sich, schmücken die Helme ihrer Helden mit Blumen und nehmen Abschied. Für diese jungen deutschen Soldaten geht es 1914 an die Front.

Des familles se réunissent, mettent des fleurs sur les casques de leurs héros avant de prendre congé, ces jeunes soldats allemands étant prêts à partir pour le front, 1914.

The United States entered the war in 1917 with orchestrated enthusiasm. Men and machines poured off the conveyor belt, as this picture of civilians being turned into 'rookies' suggests. American military propaganda was way ahead of that of other combatants.

Die USA traten 1917 mit kalkulierter Begeisterung in den Krieg ein. Männer und Ausrüstung liefen geradezu vom Fließband, wie dieses Bild von der Umwandlung von Zivilisten in „Rookies" („Frischlinge") vermuten lässt. Die amerikanische Militärpropaganda war der anderer Kriegsteilnehmer weit voraus.

L'entrée en guerre des États-Unis en 1917 est orchestrée avec un enthousiasme calculé. Les hommes et les fusils semblaient se déverser d'un tapis roulant, comme le montre ce cliché de civils transformés en « bleus ». La propagande militaire américaine était bien en avance sur celle des autres combattants.

But this photograph of a bugle boy saying goodbye to his girl is almost certainly genuine, as is her grief.

Aber diese Fotografie eines jungen Soldaten (mit Signalhorn), der seinem Mädchen Lebewohl sagt, ist mit ziemlicher Sicherheit nicht gestellt – ebenso wenig wie ihr Kummer.

Mais cette photographie montrant un clairon faisant ses adieux à sa fiancée semble véridique, de même que le chagrin de la demoiselle.

Officers on a bridge address British
soldiers after the capture of the
St Quentin Canal, 1918. After three
and a half years of trench warfare,
armies were on the move once more.

Offiziere (auf der Brücke) bei einer
Ansprache an britische Soldaten,
kurz nach der Eroberung des Kanals
von Saint-Quentin, 1918. Nach dreieinhalb Jahren Stellungskrieg kamen
die Armeen wieder in Bewegung.

Des officiers s'adressent du haut d'un
pont aux soldats britanniques après la
conquête du canal de Saint-Quentin,
en 1918. Après trois ans et demi de
guerre de tranchées, les armées
étaient à nouveau en mouvement.

In the heart of the heat, smoke and noise of battle – an American
artillery unit in action on the Western Front at the St Mihiel
Salient, a few miles south of Verdun, 27 September 1918.

Hitze, Qualm und Lärm im Herzen der Schlacht – eine amerikanische Artillerieeinheit in Aktion an der Westfront, an der
Bastionsspitze von Saint-Mihiel, ein paar Kilometer südlich
von Verdun, am 27. September 1918.

Au cœur de la tourmente, de la fumée et du bruit de la bataille
– une unité d'artillerie américaine en action sur le front Ouest
à la pointe de Saint-Mihiel, à quelques kilomètres au sud de
Verdun, le 27 septembre 1918.

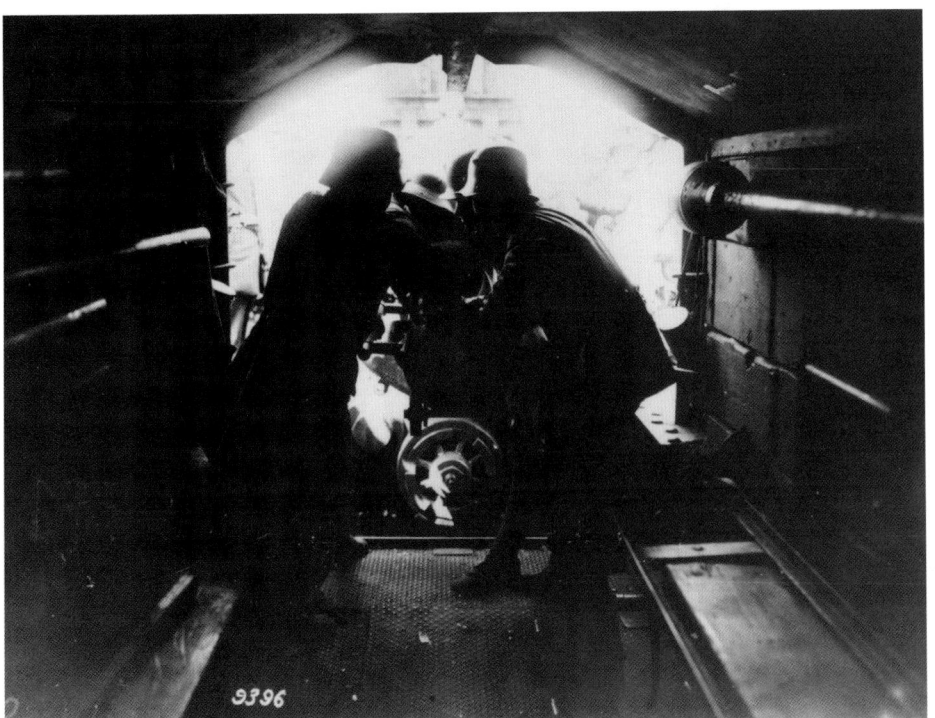

German artillerymen load shells into a gun mounted on a railway train, 1914. The original German strategy for the war was based on the Schlieffen Plan, which depended on the use of the railways of north-west Europe.

Deutsche Artilleristen bestücken ein auf einen Eisenbahnwaggon montiertes Geschütz mit Granaten, 1914. Die ursprüngliche deutsche Kriegsstrategie basierte auf dem Schlieffen-Plan, der die nordwesteuropäischen Eisenbahnen in die Planungen mit einbezog.

Des artilleurs allemands chargeant des obus dans un canon fixé sur un wagon, 1914. Le plan Schlieffen qui fut à l'origine d'une nouvelle stratégie de guerre pour les Allemands reposait sur une utilisation des chemins de fer au nord-ouest de l'Europe.

The beauty and
terror of war.
A patrol freezes as
a flare lights up
no-man's land on
the Western Front.

Schönheit und
Schrecken des Krie-
ges. Ein Patrouillen-
soldat erstarrt, als
Leuchtspurmunition
das Niemandsland
an der Westfront
erhellt.

La beauté et l'hor-
reur de la guerre.
Un patrouilleur
s'immobilise alors
qu'une fusée
éclairante illumine
un no man's land
sur le front Ouest.

A tank looms over a shell crater on the Western Front, 1917. The new machine struck terror into the hearts of its occupants as well as the enemy. It was a shock weapon, but its ability to inflict damage was limited.

Ein Panzer schwebt über einem Granattrichter an der Westfront, 1917. Das neue Gerät flößte der eigenen Besatzung ebenso viel Schrecken ein wie dem Feind. Es galt als Schockwaffe, aber seine Fähigkeit, Schaden zu stiften, hielt sich in Grenzen.

Un char surgit menaçant au-dessus d'un cratère sur le front Ouest, 1917. Cette nouvelle machine de guerre terrifiait autant ses occupants que l'ennemi. C'était une arme de choc dont la capacité de destruction était néanmoins limitée.

Big Bertha in action, 1917. The L14 Howitzer was the biggest gun in the world. It was manufactured by Krupp of Essen, had a range of 122 kilometres and bombarded Paris for more than a year and a half.

Die Dicke Bertha im Einsatz, 1917. Die L14-Haubitze war die größte Kanone der Welt. Sie wurde von Krupp in Essen hergestellt, hatte eine Reichweite von 122 Kilometern und beschoss Paris mehr als eineinhalb Jahre lang.

La grosse Bertha à l'œuvre, 1917. Fabriqué par Krupp à Essen, le Howitzer L14 fut le plus grand canon au monde. Doté d'une portée de 122 kilomètres, il fut utilisé pour bombarder Paris pendant plus d'un an et demi.

Possibly a genuine
action shot of
a German soldier
hurling a grenade,
but the figure on
the far left suggests
the photograph
was staged.

Die möglicherweise
echte Momentauf-
nahme eines deut-
schen Soldaten, der
eine Stockgranate
wirft, allerdings legt
die Gestalt links
außen nahe, dass die
Fotografie gestellt
wurde.

Cette photographie
d'un soldat allemand
lançant une grenade
semble prise sur le
vif, mais le person-
nage figurant à
l'extrême gauche du
cliché laisse penser
qu'il s'agit d'une
mise en scène.

(Above and opposite) Two scenes from the German advance at Villers-Bretonneaux, just to the east of Amiens, March 1918. (Above) A second wave of German troops passes a dead French infantryman in a shell hole.

(Oben und gegenüberliegende Seite) Zwei Szenen vom deutschen Vorstoß bei Villers-Bretonneaux, unmittelbar östlich von Amiens, im März 1918. (Oben) Eine zweite Welle deutscher Truppen passiert einen Granattrichter mit einem toten französischen Infanteristen.

(Ci-dessus et ci-contre) Deux scènes illustrant l'avancée allemande à Villers-Bretonneaux, à l'est d'Amiens, mars 1918. (Ci-dessus) Une seconde vague de soldats allemands passe devant un fantassin français tué par l'explosion d'un obus.

Ludendorff's offensive almost broke the Allied line, but it managed to hold and turn the German attack. (Above) Some of the 3 million German troops on the Western Front at this time.

Die Offensive von Ludendorff durchbrach beinahe die Linie der Alliierten. Sie hielt mit Mühe und konnte den deutschen Angriff abwehren. (Oben) Einige deutsche Soldaten aus dem Aufgebot von damals insgesamt drei Millionen an der Westfront.

La ligne des Alliés fut presque rompue par l'offensive de Ludendorff, mais elle sut résister et retourner l'attaque allemande. (Ci-dessous) Quelques-uns des trois millions de soldats allemands sur le front Ouest.

Modern warfare. German soldiers (above) create a smokescreen during the First World War. (Opposite) British casualties, blinded by gas, await treatment near Béthune, 1918.

Moderne Kriegsführung. Deutsche Soldaten (oben) verwenden künstlichen Nebel während des Ersten Weltkrieges. (Gegenüberliegende Seite) Britische Verwundete, vom Gas geblendet, warten bei Béthune darauf, behandelt zu werden, 1918.

Techniques de guerre modernes. Des soldats allemands (ci-dessus) créent un écran de brouillard durant la Première Guerre mondiale. (Ci-contre) Des blessés britanniques, rendus aveugles par les gaz, attendent d'être soignés près de Béthune, 1918.

Wounded Australian troops move back to a casualty clearing station on the Menin Road, 1917. On the outbreak of war, the Australian Prime Minister announced: 'Our duty is quite clear – to gird up our loins and remember that we are Britons.'

Verwundete australische Soldaten auf dem Rückzug erreichen ein Auffanglager des Sanitätsdienstes an der Straße nach Menin, 1917. Bei Ausbruch des Krieges verkündete der australische Premier: „Unser Auftrag ist eindeutig – uns zu rüsten und daran zu denken, dass wir Briten sind."

Des soldats australiens blessés font marche arrière vers un centre de soins sur la route de Menin, 1917. Quand la guerre fut déclarée, le Premier ministre australien déclara : « notre devoir est très simple. Il faut prendre notre courage à deux mains et ne pas oublier que nous sommes Britanniques ».

German soldiers search through the wreckage of a Red Cross truck, 1916. On both sides there were many men who refused to fight, but who died serving in non-combatant capacities.

Deutsche Soldaten durchsuchen das Wrack eines Wagens des Roten Kreuzes, 1916. Auf beiden Seiten gab es viele, die den Dienst an der Waffe verweigerten, aber in Erfüllung ihrer Pflichten bei nicht kämpfenden Truppenteilen starben.

Des soldats allemands fouillent parmi les débris d'un camion de la Croix-Rouge, en 1916. Dans les deux camps, nombreux furent les hommes qui refusèrent de combattre mais qui moururent en effectuant des opérations civiles.

The name Passchendaele passed into British military folklore as a living hell. Between July and November 1917 tens of thousands of men fought and died waist-deep in mud for possession of a few acres of derelict countryside.

Der Name Passchendaele ging als eine Hölle auf Erden in die britische Militärfolklore ein. Zwischen Juli und November 1917 kämpften und starben dort Zehntausende von Männern hüfttief im Schlamm. Es ging um einen Landgewinn von ein paar Morgen heruntergekommenen Brachlandes.

Dans le folklore militaire britannique, le nom de Passchendaele est devenu synonyme d'enfer humain. Entre juillet et novembre 1917, des dizaines de milliers d'hommes combattirent et moururent dans la boue, enfoncés jusqu'à la taille, pour conquérir quelques hectares d'une campagne ravagée.

(Opposite) A wounded soldier is carried by stretcher-bearers during the Battle of Passchendaele, 1 August 1917. (Above) Soldiers of the 16th Canadian Machine Gun Regiment in temporary defences at Passchendaele, 14 November 1917.

(Gegenüberliegende Seite) Ein Verwundeter wird bei der Schlacht um Passchendaele am 1. August 1917 auf einer Bahre weggetragen. (Oben) Soldaten des 16. Kanadischen Maschinengewehr-Regiments in provisorischen Verteidigungsstellungen bei Passchendaele, 14. November 1917.

(Ci-contre) Un soldat blessé est transporté par des brancardiers pendant la bataille de Passchendaele, 1er août 1917. (Ci-dessus) Des soldats du 16e régiment canadien des fusiliers mitrailleurs dans des postes de défense temporaires à Passchendaele, 14 novembre 1917.

Canadian troops charge into action, 1916. The first Canadian contingent arrived in Europe in October 1914, more than 30,000 of them having been recruited and trained within two months of the outbreak of war.

Kanadische Truppen stürmen 1916 in den Kampf. Das erste kanadische Kontingent traf im Oktober 1914 in Europa ein. Mehr als 30 000 Mann waren binnen zwei Monaten nach Kriegsausbruch rekrutiert und ausgebildet worden.

Soldats canadiens prêts à tirer, en 1916. Le premier contingent canadien arriva en Europe en octobre 1914, plus de 30 000 d'entre eux ayant été enrôlés et entraînés durant les deux mois qui suivirent le début de la guerre.

On the Western Front the slaughter continued unabated throughout the war. This picture of dead German troops was taken during the Battle of Cambrai at Flesquières, 23 November 1917.

Während des gesamten Krieges wurde das hemmungslose Gemetzel an der Westfront fortgesetzt. Diese Aufnahme toter deutscher Soldaten wurde während der Schlacht von Cambrai bei Flesquières am 23. November 1917 gemacht.

Sur le front Ouest, le massacre se poursuivit sans répit durant toute la guerre. Ce cliché montrant des soldats allemands morts fut pris durant la bataille de Cambrai à Flesquières, le 23 novembre 1917.

British dead, killed while covering the retreat of their colleagues during the German Spring Offensive of 1918. When the fighting finally stopped in November 1918, neither side had gained any significant ground.

Britische Soldaten, die fielen, als sie den Rückzug ihrer Truppenkameraden während der deutschen Frühjahrsoffensiven von 1918 deckten. Als die Kämpfe im November 1918 endlich eingestellt wurden, konnte keine Seite bedeutende Landgewinne vorweisen.

Soldats britanniques tués alors qu'ils couvraient la retraite de leurs camarades durant les offensives allemandes du printemps 1918. Quand la bataille cessa, en novembre 1918, aucun camp n'avait fait d'avancée significative.

Dark humour in wartime. French infantrymen use coffins as tables
while eating their dinner behind the lines, 1916. It was neither the
time nor the place for undue sensitivity.

Schwarzer Humor in Kriegszeiten. Französische Infanteristen
benutzen Särge als Esstische hinter den Linien, 1916. Für über-
triebenes Feingefühl war dies die falsche Zeit und der falsche Ort.

Humour noir en temps de guerre. À l'arrière des lignes de front,
les fantassins français prennent leurs repas sur des cercueils en
guise de tables, 1916. Ce n'était ni l'heure ni le lieu d'afficher une
sensibilité exacerbée.

The night's kill. German troops display the rats killed in their trench the previous night, March 1916. The trench appears in good condition: it is unlikely that they were reduced to eating these rodents.

Die Jagdstrecke einer Nacht. Deutsche Soldaten präsentieren im März 1916 die Ratten, die sie in der vergangenen Nacht in ihrem Schützengraben erschlagen haben. Die Stellung scheint in gutem Zustand: Es ist unwahrscheinlich, dass sie gezwungen waren, diese Nagetiere auch noch zu essen.

Conquête nocturne. Des soldats allemands présentent les rats tués dans leur tranchée la nuit précédente, mars 1916. La tranchée semble en bon état et il est donc peu probable qu'ils aient été réduits à manger ces rongeurs.

Learning his trade. Corporal Adolf Hitler (right) with two comrades in the early days of the First World War.

Lehrjahre. Der Gefreite Adolf Hitler (rechts) mit zwei Kameraden in den frühen Tagen des Ersten Weltkrieges.

Apprentissage. Le caporal Adolf Hitler (à droite) avec deux camarades au début de la Première Guerre mondiale.

Out of office.
Winston Churchill
(right), Colonel
of the Royal
Scots Fusiliers,
at Armentières,
11 February 1916.

Nicht im Amt.
Winston Churchill
(rechts), Oberst der
Royal Scots Fusiliers,
bei Armentières am
11. Februar 1916.

Au repos. Winston
Churchill (à droite),
colonel des Royal
Scots Fusiliers,
à Armentières
le 11 février 1916.

3. The home front
Die Heimatfront
Le front à domicile

A soldier on leave goes Christmas shopping with his family – a scene of 'wishful thinking'. Workers in war-related industries earned good money, but the average 'Tommy' was poorly paid.

Ein Soldat auf Heimaturlaub macht mit seiner Familie Weihnachtseinkäufe – eine Szene, die eher Wunsch als Wirklichkeit entsprach. Arbeiter in kriegswichtigen Industriezweigen verdienten gutes Geld, aber der durchschnittliche „Tommy" wurde schlecht bezahlt.

Un soldat en permission et sa famille font leurs achats de Noël – cette scène illustre bien l'adage qui dit qu'il ne faut pas prendre ses désirs pour la réalité. Les ouvriers des industries de guerre étaient bien payés tandis que le simple soldat recevait un très modeste salaire.

3. The home front
Die Heimatfront
Le front à domicile

Civilians gave flowers to departing soldiers and white feathers to those they regarded as cowards. They knitted 'comforts' for the troops and turned parks over to vegetables. They attacked the shops and businesses of enemy aliens and rushed for shelter during the intermittent air-raids.

The struggle was to maintain a semblance of 'business as usual'. Many saw it as their duty to keep theatres, dance-halls and picture palaces open; to dance and dine at fine restaurants. How else would men returning on leave from the Front have a good time and be reminded of what they were fighting for?

But the war bit savagely into the lives of everyone. Few families escaped the horror of losing a husband, a son, a brother or a father. The whole of Europe became accustomed to the living scars of war – to men who had lost their sight, their limbs, their senses.

Black marketeers 'throve like maggots in an apple'. By August 1916 there was no milk or cheese to be bought on the open market in Berlin, and butchers were offering crows, squirrels and woodpeckers for sale. The people kept on praying.

Zivilisten schenkten abreisenden Soldaten Blumen und denen, die sie als Feiglinge betrachteten, weiße Federn. Sie strickten „Nützliches" für die Truppen und verwandelten Parks in Gemüsegärten. Sie fielen über Läden und Geschäfte feindlicher Ausländer her und eilten in die Unterstände, wenn wieder einmal Luftalarm gegeben wurde.

Es ging darum, den Anschein des *business as usual* mit aller Macht aufrechtzuerhalten. Viele betrachteten es als ihre Pflicht, Theater, Tanzsäle und Kinos geöffnet zu halten, tanzen zu gehen oder in guten Restaurants zu essen. Wie sonst konnten sich die Männer auf Fronturlaub wohl fühlen und daran erinnert werden, wofür sie kämpften?

Aber der Krieg griff gnadenlos in das Leben aller ein. Wenigen Familien blieb der Schrecken erspart, einen Ehemann, einen Sohn, einen Bruder oder Vater zu verlieren. Ganz Europa musste sich an die lebenden Wundmale des Krieges gewöhnen – an Männer, die ihr Augenlicht, ihre Glieder, ihren Verstand verloren hatten.

Schwarzmarkthändler lebten „wie die Made im Speck". Schon im August 1916 war in Berlin keine Milch und kein Käse mehr auf dem offiziellen Markt erhältlich, und die Metzger boten Krähen, Eichhörnchen und Spechte zum Verkauf. Die Menschen hörten nicht auf zu beten.

Les civils distribuèrent des fleurs aux soldats qui partaient à la guerre et des plumes blanches à ceux qu'ils considéraient être des lâches. Ils tricotèrent des « mascottes » pour les soldats et transformèrent les parcs en potagers. Ils attaquèrent les commerces et les entreprises qui appartenaient aux étrangers ennemis de la patrie et coururent aux abris durant les raids aériens sporadiques.

Malgré les tristes circonstances, il fallait s'efforcer de maintenir un semblant de « tout va très bien, Madame la Marquise ». Beaucoup d'individus estimaient, en effet, qu'il était de leur devoir de garder les théâtres, les salles de bal et les cinémas ouverts, d'aller manger et danser dans d'excellents restaurants. Autrement, comment les hommes de retour du front pour une permission auraient-ils pu vraiment s'amuser et se rappeler les raisons de leur engagement ?

Mais la guerre mordit sauvagement dans la vie de chacun. Peu de familles échappèrent à l'horreur de perdre un mari, un fils, un frère ou un père. Toute l'Europe dut s'habituer aux plaies vivantes de la guerre et à ces hommes qui avaient perdu la vue, un membre ou la raison.

Les profiteurs du marché noir grouillaient comme les vers dans la pomme. En août 1916, il n'était plus possible d'acheter du lait ou du fromage dans les magasins de Berlin et les bouchers vendaient sur leurs étals des corbeaux, des écureuils et des piverts. Les gens continuaient à prier.

The queue for the air-raid shelter, Hither Green, London, October 1917. Bombing raids by Zeppelins were becoming more frequent by now.

Schlange stehen am Luftschutzbunker, Hither Green, London, im Oktober 1917. Bombenangriffe von Zeppelinen wurden jetzt häufiger.

Queue pour se réfugier dans un abri antiaérien à Hither Green (Londres), octobre 1917. À cette époque, les bombardements effectués par des Zeppelins devenaient de plus en plus fréquents.

A woman munitions worker at Vickers, 1915. Most women preferred such work to domestic service. 'It was much more comfortable, it was more money… I was on two or three pounds a week… with all the girls it was like a jolly party' – Lil Truphet.

Eine Munitionsarbeiterin in den Vickers-Werken, 1915. Die meisten Frauen zogen solche Arbeit dem Haushalt vor. „Es war viel leichter, es bedeutete mehr Geld … ich hatte zwei oder drei Pfund die Woche … mit all den anderen Mädels war es wie eine richtig fröhliche Gesellschaft" – Lil Truphet.

Ouvrière d'une usine de munitions à Vickers, 1915. La majorité des femmes préféraient ce travail aux tâches ménagères. « C'était bien mieux, ça rapportait plus d'argent … Moi, je gagnais deux à trois livres par semaine … et, nous les filles, on s'amusait tout le temps " – Lil Truphet.

A recruiting march through London by members of the Women's Auxiliary Army Corps, 1915. For young women, the armed forces offered a more exciting life and greater freedom than they would have enjoyed at home.

Ein Rekrutierungsmarsch von Mitgliedern des Women's Auxiliary Army Corps (Weibliches Armee-Hilfskorps) in London, 1915. Jungen Frauen boten die Streitkräfte ein aufregenderes Leben und größere Freiheiten als ein Leben daheim.

Marche pour la mobilisation organisée par le corps des femmes auxiliaires de l'armée à travers Londres, 1915. Pour les jeunes femmes, l'armée offrait une vie plus trépidante et une liberté plus grande que tout ce qu'elles auraient connu en restant au foyer.

Public disgrace. A conscientious objector is made to sit in specially built stocks, 1916. Painted on the seat is the slogan 'This is for traitors'. Conscription had come to Britain for the first time.

Öffentliche Bloßstellung. Ein Kriegsdienstverweigerer wird 1916 an den eigens konstruierten Pranger gestellt. Die Inschrift auf der Lehne des Sitzes lautet: „Das ist der Lohn für Verräter". Erstmals gab es in Großbritannien die allgemeine Wehrpflicht.

Disgrâce publique. Un objecteur de conscience est mis au pilori sur un banc construit à cet effet, 1916. Le slogan peint sur le dossier dit « Pour les traîtres ». C'était la première fois que la conscription était obligatoire en Grande-Bretagne.

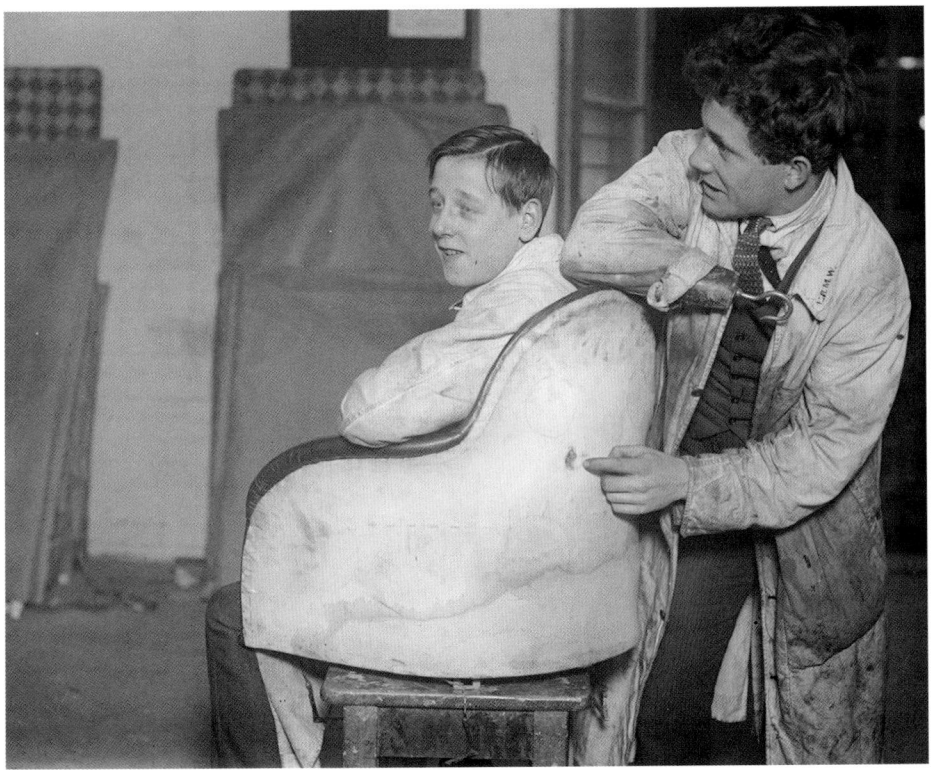

Private disability. Two limbless ex-servicemen examine the seat from a German Gotha bomber at Lord Roberts' Memorial Workshop in the Brompton Road, London, December 1917.

Behindert. Zwei Exsoldaten mit amputierten Gliedmaßen prüfen den Sitz eines deutschen Gotha-Bombers in Lord Robert's Memorial Workshop in der Brompton Road, London, Dezember 1917.

Infirmité personnelle. Deux ex-soldats amputés examinent le siège d'un bombardier allemand Gotha exposé au Lord Robert's Memorial Workshop à Brompton Road (Londres), en décembre 1917.

Lady Diana Manners (in nurse's uniform) collects funds for 'Our Day', 19 October 1916. The British army had just suffered its worst ever losses in battle. The aim of the collection was to provide food and tobacco for the survivors.

Lady Diana Manners (in Schwesterntracht) sammelt Spenden bei der Aktion „Our Day", 19. Oktober 1916. Die britische Armee hatte gerade die schlimmsten Kriegsverluste aller Zeiten erlitten. Ziel der Sammlung war es, Lebensmittel und Tabak für die Überlebenden bereitzustellen.

Lady Diana Manners (en blouse d'infirmière) collecte des dons pour la journée intitulée « Our Day », le 19 octobre 1916. L'armée britannique venait d'enregistrer les plus graves pertes jamais subies jusque-là. Le but de la collecte était de fournir des repas et du tabac aux survivants.

Soldiers and sailors attend the mass funeral of victims of the *Lusitania* disaster, May 1915. The sinking of the Cunard liner by German torpedoes, with the loss of 1,198 lives, provided a propaganda coup for the British Government.

Soldaten und Matrosen beim Massenbegräbnis von Opfern der *Lusitania*-Katastrophe im Mai 1915. Die Versenkung des Passagierschiffes der Cunard-Linie durch deutsche Torpedos, bei der 1198 Menschen ihr Leben verloren, gab der britischen Regierung Anlass zu einem Propagandafeldzug.

Soldats et marins participant aux funérailles collectives des victimes du désastre du *Lusitania*, mai 1915. Le naufrage du paquebot Cunard, qui fut torpillé par les Allemands et causa la mort de 1198 personnes, fut un énorme coup de propagande pour le gouvernement britannique.

The fruits of Empire. During a potato shortage, a market trader offers pineapples as an alternative, 1 February 1917. How many takers he found at ninepence (4p) each, we do not know.

Die Früchte des Empire. Während eines Engpasses in der Kartoffel-versorgung bietet dieser Händler auf dem Markt Ananas als Alternative an, 1. Februar 1917. Wie viele Käufer er bei einem Stückpreis von Ninepence (damals etwa 75 Pfennig) fand, wissen wir nicht.

Les fruits de l'Empire. Un marchand de légumes vend des ananas, faute de pommes de terre, 1ᵉʳ février 1917. Reste à savoir combien il trouva d'acheteurs à neuf pence la pièce.

The seeds of hope. London and South West railwaymen head for railway waste ground to plant their sacks of seed potatoes, April 1917. Golf courses and even cricket fields became vegetable gardens during the war.

Die Saat der Hoffnung. Eisenbahner aus London und dem Südwesten auf dem Weg zu Brachland im Besitz der Eisenbahn, wo sie mit dem Saatgut aus den Säcken neue Kartoffelfelder anlegen wollen, April 1917. Während des Krieges wurden Golfplätze und sogar Kricketfelder zu Gemüseplantagen.

Les graines de l'espoir. Des cheminots de Londres et du Sud-Ouest se dirigent vers les terrains vagues des voies ferrées pour y planter des pommes de terre, avril 1917. Les terrains de golf et même les terrains de cricket furent transformés en potagers durant la guerre.

Voluntary workers at the British War Library pack parcels of books to be despatched to troops on active service, 24 August 1916. Reading helped combat the boredom of trench warfare.

Freiwillige in der britischen Kriegsbücherei helfen beim Packen von Buchpaketen, die dann an die kämpfenden Truppen verschickt werden, 24. August 1916. Lektüre half beim Kampf gegen die Langeweile im Grabenkrieg.

Des bénévoles de la Bibliothèque militaire britannique font des paquets de livres destinés aux soldats en service, 24 août 1916. Lire était un moyen de combattre l'ennui de la guerre des tranchées.

Assembling parcels of food and other comforts for British prisoners of war in Germany, 1916. 'Other comforts' might include clothing, games, books and magazines, and – on at least one occasion – cricket balls.

Pakete mit Lebensmitteln und anderen Hilfsgütern für britische Kriegsgefangene in Deutschland werden zusammengestellt, 1916. „Andere Hilfsgüter" konnte Kleidungsstücke, Spiele, Bücher und Zeitschriften oder – zumindest bei einer Gelegenheit – Kricketbälle bedeuten.

Confection de paquets de nourriture et autres commodités pour les prisonniers britanniques détenus en Allemagne, 1916. « Autres commodités » signifiaient, par exemple, des habits, des jeux, des livres, des revues et même, en tout cas au moins une fois, des balles de cricket.

Wounded soldiers, wearing a new type of crutch fitted to the belt, attempt to topple a 'Kokonut Kaiser' at a fair in Sidcup, Kent, 1 September 1917. Much wry humour and hatred was directed towards the German Emperor during the war.

Kriegsversehrte mit einer neuen Art von Krücke, die um die Hüfte geschnallt wurde, versuchen auf einem Jahrmarkt in Sidcup, Kent, am 1. September 1917, einen „Kokosnuss-Kaiser" über den Haufen zu werfen. Während des Krieges richtete sich sehr viel sarkastischer Humor und Hass gegen den deutschen Kaiser.

Des soldats blessés, équipés d'un nouveau type de béquilles fixées à la ceinture, tentent de renverser l'empereur au jeu de massacre sur une foire à Sidcup (Kent), 1ᵉʳ septembre 1917. Durant la guerre, l'Empereur allemand fut l'objet de nombreuses plaisanteries ironiques voire haineuses.

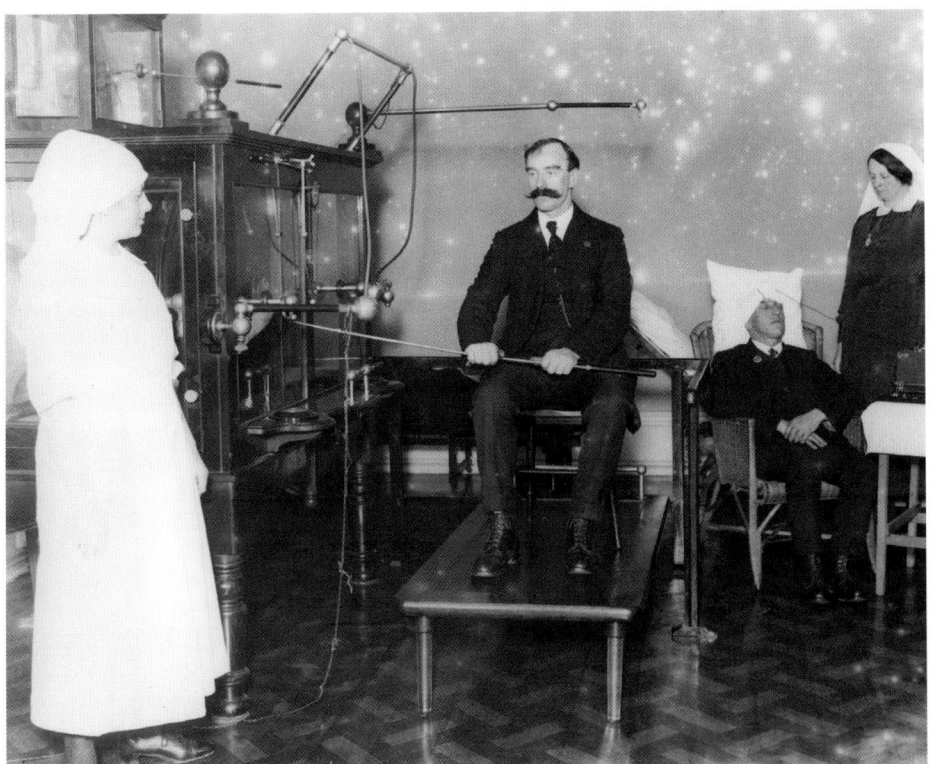

Nurses at a hospital in Britain superintend the use of experimental new apparatus for soldiers suffering from shell-shock, 1917. It took a long time for the medical profession to accept that such a condition was genuine.

Schwestern in einem britischen Krankenhaus beaufsichtigen die Anwendung eines neuen Gerätes gegen die Kriegsneurose, 1917. Der medizinische Berufsstand brauchte lange, um zu erkennen, dass es sich dabei um eine wirkliche Krankheit handelte.

Des infirmières d'un hôpital britannique surveillent l'utilisation d'appareils expérimentaux destinés aux soldats traumatisés par des éclatements d'obus, 1917. La profession médicale mit longtemps à reconnaître qu'un tel état de choc n'était pas factice.

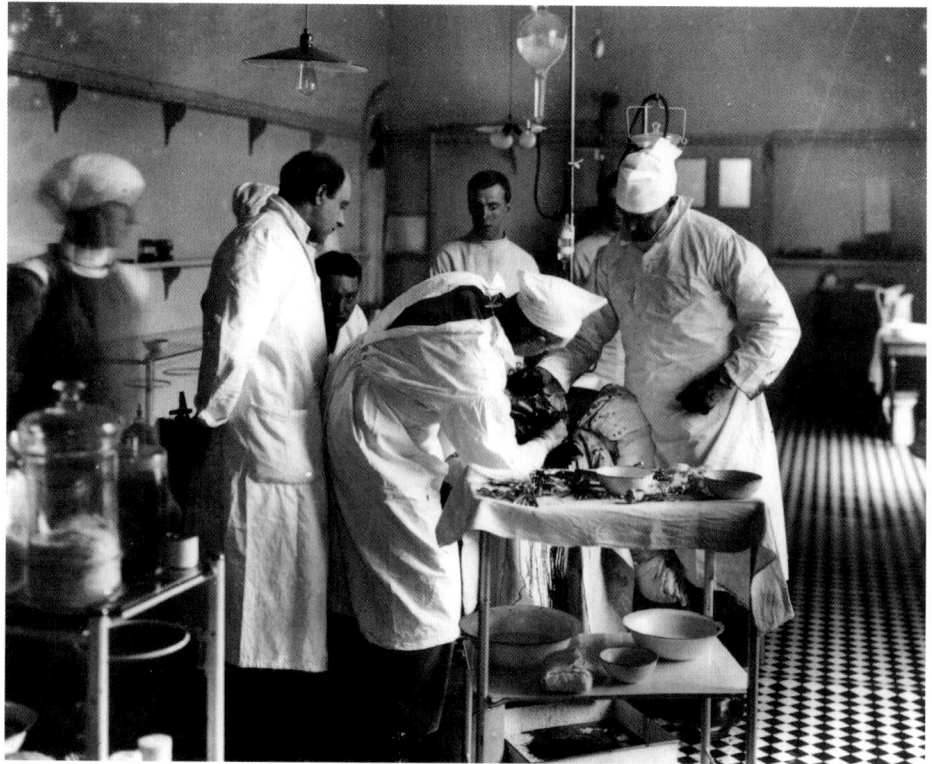

An amputation in progress at the Duchess of Westminster Military Hospital, 1915. The route from battlefield to well-equipped hospital for such an operation was often a slow and painful one.

Im Militärkrankenhaus Duchess of Westminster wird eine Amputation vorgenommen, 1915. Der Weg vom Schlachtfeld zu einem für solche Operationen gut ausgerüsteten Lazarett war häufig lang und mühsam.

Amputation en cours à l'hôpital militaire Duchess of Westminster, 1915. Le trajet du champ de bataille à un hôpital bien équipé pour ce genre d'opération était souvent long et douloureux.

Soldiers attend a charity concert at the Savoy Hotel, London, March 1916. Privately, many hoped for a 'Blighty' wound – one serious enough for them to be sent home, but not permanently disabling. Few were so lucky.

Soldaten bei einem Wohltätigkeitskonzert im Savoy Hotel, London, März 1916. Insgeheim hofften viele auf eine „Heimatverwundung" – schwer genug, um nach Hause geschickt zu werden, aber doch nicht so schwer, dass sie bleibende Schäden hinterließ. Wenige hatten dieses Glück.

Soldats à un concert de charité au Savoy Hotel à Londres en mars 1916. En leur for intérieur, beaucoup espéraient se voir infliger une blessure « à l'Angleterre », c'est-à-dire une blessure assez grave pour justifier un retour au pays, mais pas assez grave pour rester handicapé à vie. Ils furent peu nombreux à avoir cette chance.

Playing at soldiers. The Lord Mayor of London (third from left) and his officials visit the mock-up of a trench at an Active Services Exhibition in Knightsbridge, London, March 1916.

Soldat spielen. Der Oberbürgermeister von London (Dritter von links) und seine offiziellen Begleiter besuchen den Nachbau eines Schützengrabens bei einer Ausstellung der Streitkräfte in Knightsbridge, London, März 1916.

Jouer aux soldats. Monsieur le maire de Londres (troisième à gauche) et ses adjoints visitent une reconstitution de tranchée dans le cadre d'une exposition sur les champs d'honneur à Knightsbrigdge (Londres), mars 1916.

Soldiers at play. American troops enjoy donkey rides on the sands at Southport, Lancashire, 6 June 1918. From June 1917 they arrived in Europe at the rate of 50,000 every month.

Spielende Soldaten. Amerikanische Truppen genießen einen Eselausritt am Sandstrand von Southport, Lancashire, am 6. Juni 1918. Ab Juni 1917 trafen allmonatlich 50 000 von ihnen in Europa ein.

Soldats en train de jouer. Des militaires américains s'amusent à monter des ânes sur la plage de Southport (Lancashire), 6 juin 1918. Dès juin 1917, ils débarquèrent en Europe au rythme de 50 000 hommes par mois.

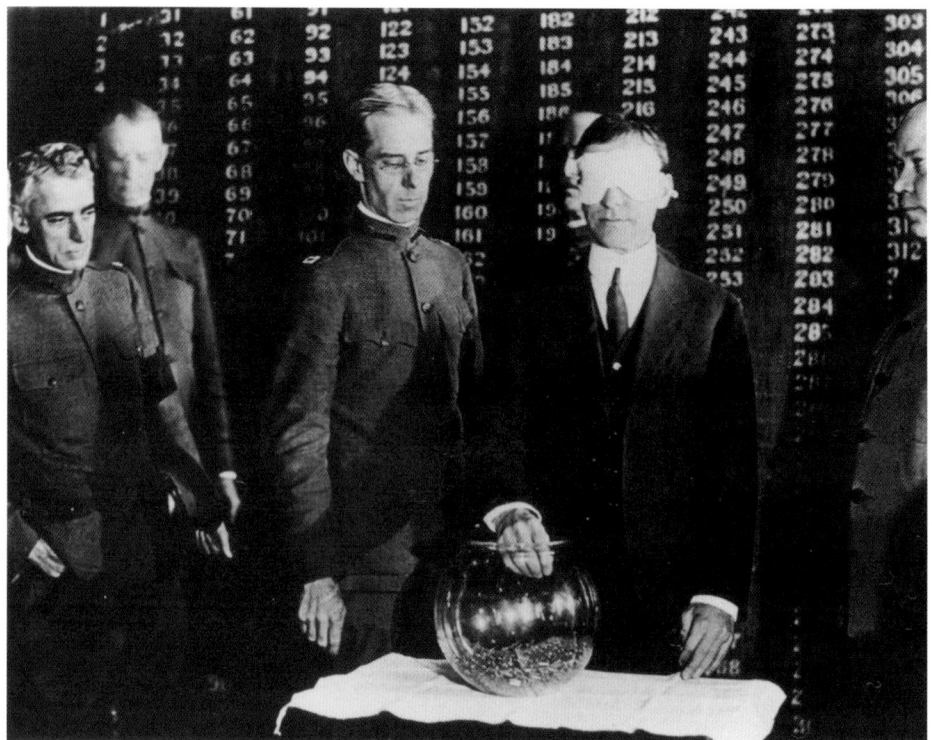

Under the terms of the Selective Draft Act of May 1917 every American male
between 21 and 30 years old had to register for national service. Each was given
a number. Here the numbers of those to be drafted are picked by lottery.

Nach Maßgabe des „Gesetzes zur selektiven Aushebung" von Mai 1917 musste sich
jeder männliche Amerikaner im Alter zwischen 21 und 30 Jahren zum Wehrdienst
registrieren lassen. Jedem wurde eine Zahl zugeteilt. Hier wird im Lotterieverfahren
ermittelt, wer eingezogen wird.

Conformément à la loi de conscription obligatoire de mai 1917, tous les Américains
âgés de 21 à 30 ans étaient obligés de s'enrôler dans l'armée et recevaient un numéro.
Ce cliché montre le tirage au sort des numéros de ceux qui seront mobilisés.

Americans are encouraged to sign a Declaration of Patriotism following the United States' decision to enter the war, April 1917.

Nach der Entscheidung der Vereinigten Staaten für den Kriegseintritt im April 1917 werden die Amerikaner aufgefordert, eine „patriotische Erklärung" zu unterzeichnen.

Les Américains sont encouragés à signer une « Déclaration de patriotisme » après la décision des États-Unis d'entrer en guerre, avril 1917.

Although it had been proved that the cavalry had little part to play in modern warfare, a squadron of American cavalrymen show their horsemanship, 1917. The days of Teddy Roosevelt's Rough Riders were over.

Wenn auch erwiesen war, dass die Kavallerie im modernen Krieg keine große Rolle spielte, zeigt hier eine Schwadron amerikanischer Kavalleristen ihre Reitkünste, 1917. Die Tage der „Wilden Reiter" des Teddy Roosevelt waren vorüber.

Bien que l'on sache que la cavalerie n'aurait plus de rôle important à jouer dans une guerre moderne, ces cavaliers américains font néanmoins la démonstration de leur virtuosité équestre, 1917. Le temps des Rough Riders de Teddy Roosevelt était révolu.

A group of black GIs, 1918. There were many whites in the United States who frowned upon the idea of arming African-Americans, and many blacks who disliked the idea of fighting the white man's war. In the end, more than 400,000 blacks enlisted.

Eine Gruppe schwarzer GIs 1918. Viele Weiße in den USA hatten etwas dagegen, Afroamerikanern Waffen in die Hand zu geben, und viele Schwarze mochten den Gedanken nicht, sich am Krieg des weißen Mannes zu beteiligen. Schließlich ließen sich mehr als 400 000 Schwarze rekrutieren.

Groupe de G.I. noirs, 1918. Aux États-Unis, les Blancs furent nombreux à s'opposer au principe d'armer les Afro-américains. Quant aux Noirs, ils furent tout aussi nombreux à désapprouver le fait de se battre dans une guerre de Blancs. Finalement, plus de 400 000 Noirs s'enrôlèrent.

Cossack soldiers stroll through the streets of London, 1916. One of the early myths of the war was that an army of Cossacks had passed through England one night on their way to the Western Front 'with snow on their boots'.

Kosaken spazieren 1916 durch die Londoner Straßen. Einer frühen Kriegslegende zufolge durchquerte eines Nachts eine Kosakenarmee auf dem Weg zur Westfront England „mit Schnee an den Stiefeln".

Des cosaques en promenade dans les rues de Londres, en 1916. Selon un des premiers mythes de la guerre, une nuit une armée de cosaques « avec de la neige sur leurs bottes » traversa l'Angleterre pour rejoindre le front Ouest.

A crowd gathers outside a small shop in the East End of London, June 1915. The owners have painted 'We are Russians' on the shop front, to protect themselves from anti-German vandalism.

Eine Menschenansammlung vor einem kleinen Laden im Londoner East End, Juni 1915. Die Besitzer haben „Wir sind Russen" auf die Fassade gemalt, um sich vor antideutschem Vandalismus zu schützen.

Badauds assemblés devant une petite boutique dans l'East End (Londres), juin 1915. Les propriétaires ont peint « nous sommes russes » sur la devanture afin de se protéger des actes de vandalisme anti-allemands.

4. The wider war
Der Krieg in seiner ganzen Ausdehnung
La guerre dans le monde

Russian prisoners of war are marched away after their defeat at the Masurian Lakes in East Prussia, May 1915. From the very beginning of the war, the Russian army was ill-clad and ill-equipped.

Russische Kriegsgefangene werden nach ihrer Niederlage auf der Masurischen Seenplatte in Ostpreußen im Mai 1915 abgeführt. Seit Kriegsanfang war die russische Armee schlecht gekleidet und schlecht ausgerüstet.

Retrait des prisonniers russes après leur défaite aux lacs de Mazurie en Prusse-Orientale. Dès le début de la guerre, l'armée russe fut mal habillée et mal équipée.

4. The wider war
Der Krieg in seiner ganzen Ausdehnung
La guerre dans le monde

More than 10 million men were killed in the First World War. Another 21 million were wounded. Although the Western Front was the most concentrated area of slaughter, losses on the Eastern Front were as great. Men died as far south as the Falkland Islands, as far north as the Arctic Circle. They died off the eastern seaboard of the United States and in the heat and dust of Mesopotamia. Gunboats engaged each other in Pacific atolls and in the creeks of Africa. It was the worst global catastrophe since the Black Death in the 1340s.

Men came from all over to the fields of carnage: Australians and New Zealanders died at Gallipoli; Canadians heroically stormed Vimy Ridge. Turkish soldiers fought a *jihad*, a Muslim holy war, against the infidels in Syria, bombarding thousands of Indian troops in the British garrison at Kut. The army which General Allenby led into Jerusalem included men from Singapore, Hong Kong and the West Indies.

In Europe few countries escaped active involvement. Men died in Hungary, Serbia, Italy, Romania, Bulgaria, Poland, Russia and a dozen other principalities. The contagion of madness was complete. War touched and contaminated every continent in the world.

Mehr als 10 Millionen Menschen kamen im Ersten Weltkrieg ums Leben. Weitere 21 Millionen wurden verwundet. Die meisten Schlachten fanden zwar an der Westfront statt, die Verluste an der Ostfront waren aber genauso groß. Männer starben tief im Süden auf den Falklandinseln und weit im Norden am Polarkreis. Sie starben vor der Ostküste der Vereinigten Staaten und in der Hitze und dem Staub Mesopotamiens. Kanonenboote bekriegten einander bei pazifischen Atollen und in den Buchten Afrikas. Es war die größte weltumspannende Katastrophe seit dem schwarzen Tod in den 1340er Jahren.

Männer kamen von überall her zu den Stätten des Blutbades: Australier und Neuseeländer starben bei Gallipoli; Kanadier erstürmten heroisch die Höhen von Vimy. Türkische Soldaten kämpften den Dschihad, den islamischen heiligen Krieg, gegen die Ungläubigen in Syrien und bombardierten Tausende indischer Soldaten in der britischen Garnison bei Kut. Die Armee, die General Allenby nach Jerusalem führte, bestand aus Soldaten aus Singapur, Hongkong und von den Antillen.

In Europa waren nur wenige Länder nicht direkt am Krieg beteiligt. Männer starben in Ungarn, Serbien, Italien, Rumänien, Bulgarien, Polen, Russland und einem Dutzend weiterer Fürstenreiche. Der Irrsinn war hochansteckend. Der Krieg berührte und verseuchte jeden Kontinent der Welt.

La Première Guerre mondiale tua plus de 10 millions d'hommes et fit 21 millions de blessés. Bien que les massacres convergèrent essentiellement sur le front Ouest, les pertes humaines engendrées sur le front Est furent tout aussi énormes. Des hommes moururent à l'extrême sud de la Terre, sur les îles Falkland et dans le cercle arctique. D'autres perdirent la vie sur les côtes orientales des États-Unis et dans la chaleur et la poussière de la Mésopotamie. Des canonnières franchirent les atolls du Pacifique et les criques africaines. Ce fut la catastrophe mondiale la plus meurtrière depuis la peste noire des années 1340.

Des hommes venus de partout se retrouvèrent sur les champs de bataille : des Australiens et des Néo-Zélandais moururent à Gallipoli, des Canadiens conquirent héroïquement Vimy Ridge. Des soldats turcs menèrent une *jihad*, la guerre sainte islamique, contre les infidèles de Syrie en bombardant des milliers de soldats indiens de la garnison britannique à Kut. L'armée qui pénétra dans Jérusalem, conduite par le Général Allenby, comptait dans ses rangs des hommes venus de Singapour, de Hong-Kong et des Antilles.

En Europe, rares furent les pays qui ne furent pas impliqués directement dans le conflit. Des hommes moururent en Hongrie, en Serbie, Italie, Roumanie, Bulgarie, Pologne, Russie et une douzaine d'autres principautés. La contagion de la folie fut générale. La guerre toucha et contamina tous les continents du monde.

Russian gunners work their light field guns in direct line-of-sight formation on the Eastern Front, 1914.

Russische Artilleristen bringen an der Ostfront ihre leichten Feldhaubitzen in Position, 1914.

Des artilleurs russes manoeuvrent leur canon de campagne pour viser tout droit sur le front Est, 1914.

A Russian regimental band accompanies troops to the Front, 23 June 1915. Most regiments had their own band and their own priest. Which of the two did more for morale is unknown.

Ein russisches Musikkorps begleitet Soldaten an die Front, 23. Juni 1915. Die meisten Regimenter hatten eine eigene Musikkapelle und einen eigenen Priester. Was der Hebung der Moral mehr diente, bleibt dahingestellt.

Fanfare d'un régiment russe accompagnant les soldats sur le front, 23 juin 1915. La plupart des régiments avaient leur propre fanfare et prêtre. On ne se posait pas la question de savoir lequel des deux était meilleur pour le moral …

A unit of Cossack infantry on the march, 1915. Many Russian regiments traditionally had at least one boy-soldier as a mascot, but all-out modern warfare was no place for mascots.

Aufmarsch einer Kosakeninfanterieeinheit, 1915. Viele russische Regimenter hatten traditionell einen Knaben in Uniform als Maskottchen dabei, aber der uneingeschränkte moderne Krieg ließ Maskottchen keinen Platz.

Unité d'infanterie cosaque en marche, 1915. Traditionnellement, les régiments russes avaient au moins un enfant soldat comme mascotte, mais la guerre totale moderne ne devait plus laisser de place à ces mascottes.

German troops
block railway lines
on the Eastern
Front, 1917. At this
stage of the war they
were looking for
bands of pillaging
irregular soldiers.

Deutsche Truppen
blockieren 1917
Eisenbahngleise an
der Ostfront. In
dieser Phase des
Krieges suchten
sie nach Banden
marodierender
Soldaten.

Soldats allemands
bloquant des voies
ferrées sur le front
Est, 1917. À ce stade
de la guerre, ils
recherchaient les
soldats maraudeurs
qui se livraient
occasionnellement à
du pillage en bande.

In the last days of the war in the east, a Russian soldier equipped
with full anti-gas apparatus advances across no-man's land, 1917.
The Tsar had already abdicated: the end was near for his armies.

In den letzten Kriegstagen im Osten rückt ein russischer Soldat in
voller Giftgasmontur im Niemandsland vor, 1917. Der Zar hatte
bereits abgedankt: Für seine Armeen war das Ende in Sicht.

À quelques jours de la fin de la guerre à l'est, un soldat russe
équipé d'un masque à gaz complet s'aventure dans le no man's
land, 1917. Le tsar avait déjà abdiqué, la fin approchait pour
ses armées.

German soldiers enter the looted and burning town of Szawle, 1918. The war was officially over in the east, but years were to pass before law and order returned to the region.

Deutsche Soldaten rücken in die geplünderte und brennende Stadt Szawle ein, 1918. Der Krieg im Osten war offiziell vorüber, aber Jahre sollten vergehen, bevor Recht und Ordnung in der Region wiederhergestellt waren.

Les soldats allemands entrent dans la ville de Szawle livrée au pillage et aux flammes, 1918. Officiellement, la guerre à l'Est était terminée, mais il fallut attendre des années avant que le droit et l'ordre ne soient restaurés dans cette région du monde.

Russian troops throw down their guns and surrender, 1917. To the front was the German army, to the rear a divided country. They had little alternative.

Russische Truppen legen die Gewehre nieder und ergeben sich, 1917. Vor ihnen stand die deutsche Armee, hinter ihnen lag ein zerrissenes Land. Ihnen blieb kaum eine Alternative.

Des soldats russes jettent leurs armes et se rendent, 1917. Devant eux, il y avait l'armée allemande et, derrière eux, un pays divisé. Ils n'avaient guère le choix.

In the wake of the Russian Revolution, Finnish Communists and Social Democrats rose against their right-wing government in January 1918. An all-out civil war followed, in which whole towns were destroyed.

Im Kielwasser der Russischen Revolution erhoben sich finnische Kommunisten und Sozialdemokraten im Januar 1918 gegen ihre rechtsgerichtete Regierung. Es folgte ein regelrechter Bürgerkrieg, in dem ganze Städte zerstört wurden.

Dans le sillon de la révolution russe, les communistes et sociaux-démocrates finlandais se soulevèrent contre leur gouvernement conservateur en janvier 1918. Une guerre civile totale s'ensuivit, causant la destruction de villes entières.

'White' counter-revolutionary prisoners of the Red Guard are marched down the street. The rising was eventually crushed by White Army troops, and some 23,000 'Reds' were killed.

„Weiße" konterrevolutionäre Gefangene der Roten Garden werden auf der Straße abgeführt. Der Aufstand wurde schließlich von der Weißen Armee niedergeschlagen und gut 23 000 „Rote" wurden umgebracht.

Des contre-révolutionnaires 'blancs', prisonniers de la garde Rouge, sont emmenés à pied dans la rue. Le soulèvement fut finalement réprimé par les soldats de l'armée blanche et près de 23 000 « Rouges » furent tués.

A quiet day at Anzac Cove on
the Gallipoli Peninsula, 1915.
The campaign was one of the most
ill-conceived of the war.

Ein ruhiger Tag in der Anzac-Bucht
auf der Halbinsel Gallipoli, 1915.
Der Feldzug gehörte zu den am
schlechtesten geplanten des Krieges.

Journée de repos à Anzac Cove
dans la péninsule de Gallipoli, 1915.
Cette campagne fut l'une des plus
mal conçues de la guerre.

Ernest Brooks's
photograph of a
60-pounder
heavy field
gun bombarding
Turkish positions at
Helles Bay, Gallipoli
(Gelibolu), 1915.

Ernest Brooks' Auf-
nahme eines schwe-
ren 60-Pfünder-Feld-
geschützes bei der
Bombardierung tür-
kischer Stellungen
am Kap Helles,
Gallipoli (Gelibolu),
1915.

Canon de 60 livres
bombardant les
positions turques
dans la Baie de
Helles à Gallipoli,
photographié par
Ernest Brooks, 1915.

Fires destroy a section of the city of Constantinople, 1916. Britain confidently expected to capture the city but never did. It was occupied by British troops, however, after the war.

Brände zerstören einen Teil von Konstantinopel, 1916. Großbritannien war sich sicher, die Stadt einnehmen zu können, tat es aber nie. Sie wurde allerdings nach dem Krieg von britischen Truppen besetzt.

Des incendies détruisirent une partie de Constantinople, 1916. La Grande-Bretagne, qui était certaine de pouvoir s'emparer de la ville, n'y parvint jamais. Par contre, la ville fut occupée par les soldats britanniques après la guerre.

Turkish troops undergoing training. Despite occasional debacles and some appalling leadership, the fighting qualities of the Turkish armies were much respected by Allied soldiers.

Türkische Soldaten in der Ausbildung. Trotz gelegentlicher Debakel und einigen schweren Mängeln in der Führung wurden die Kampfqualitäten der türkischen Armeen von den alliierten Soldaten mit großem Respekt betrachtet.

Soldats turcs à l'entraînement. À l'exception de débâcles occasionnelles et de quelques dirigeants désastreux, les armées turques étaient très respectées par les soldats alliés pour leurs aptitudes au combat.

(Opposite) Perhaps the most romantic figure of the war – T E Lawrence, in Arab dress, 1918. (Above) Lawrence of Arabia with his guerrilla troops in the desert, July 1917.

(Gegenüberliegende Seite) Vielleicht die romantischste Gestalt des Krieges – T. E. Lawrence, in arabischer Kleidung, 1918. (Oben) Lawrence von Arabien mit seiner Guerillatruppe in der Wüste, Juli 1917.

(Ci-contre) Probablement le personnage le plus romantique de la guerre, T. E. Lawrence, vêtu comme les Arabes, 1918. (Ci-dessus) Lawrence d'Arabie et son armée de guérilleros dans le désert, juillet 1917.

A British officer poses with his Japanese counterpart beside a heavily camouflaged gun, at Tsingtao (now Qingdao), China, on the Yellow Sea, 1914. Britain maintained a military presence in the Far East.

Ein britischer Offizier posiert mit seinem japanischen Gegenüber vor einem vorbildlich getarnten Geschütz in Tsingtao (heute Ching-Tao), China, am Gelben Meer, 1914. Großbritannien blieb weiterhin im Fernen Osten militärisch präsent.

Un officier britannique pose avec ses alter ego japonais devant un canon bien camouflé, à Tsingtao (aujourd'hui Qingdao) en Chine, sur les bords de la mer Jaune, 1914. La Grande-Bretagne maintint une présence militaire en Extrême-Orient.

A wounded orderly from the Royal Army Medical Corps is carried on a Chinese wheelbarrow, Tsingtao, China, 1914. He was a victim of one of the last colonial actions in this part of the world.

Ein verwundeter Sanitäter des Royal Army Medical Corps wird auf einer chinesischen Schubkarre weggefahren, Tsingtao, China, 1914. Er wurde das Opfer eines der letzten kolonialen Zusammenstöße in diesem Teil der Welt.

Un secouriste blessé appartenant au corps médical de la Royal Army est évacué sur une charrue chinoise à Tsingtao en Chine, 1914. Il fut la victime de l'une des dernières actions coloniales entreprises dans cette partie du monde.

Serbian troops test the accuracy of captured Austrian rifles, Belgrade, 1915.
The spark that had set the world ablaze at Sarajevo a year earlier was steadily
destroying the Austro-Hungarian Empire.

Serbische Soldaten prüfen die Präzision erbeuteter österreichischer Gewehre,
Belgrad, 1915. Der Funke, der die Welt im Jahr zuvor in Sarajewo entzündet
hatte, zerstörte unaufhaltsam die k. u. k. Monarchie.

Des soldats serbes testent la précision des fusils autrichiens qu'ils ont saisis,
Belgrade, 1915. L'étincelle qui avait mis le feu au monde à Sarajevo un an
plus tôt détruisait progressivement l'Empire austro-hongrois.

A Serbian soldier is given a shave in the trenches. This was one of several pictures from a series called 'Scenes with our Serbian Allies', published in Britain. The Serbs were regarded as gallant fighters and steadfast allies.

Ein serbischer Soldat wird im Schützengraben rasiert. Dieses Bild stammt aus einer Serie mit dem Titel „Bei unseren serbischen Alliierten", die in Großbritannien veröffentlicht wurde. Die Serben wurden als edle Kämpfer und standhafte Bundesgenossen betrachtet.

Séance de rasage pour un soldat serbe dans une tranchée. Ce cliché faisait partie d'une série intitulée « La vie avec nos alliés serbes », publiée en Grande-Bretagne. Les Serbes étaient considérés comme de galants combattants et de loyaux alliés.

5. Air and sea
Zu Wasser und in der Luft
Ciel et mer

A British battle squadron ploughs through an Atlantic swell,
September 1914. In the foreground are the guns of HMS *Audacious*.
Britannia, it appears, still rules the waves.

Ein britisches Kampfgeschwader kämpft sich im Atlantik durch
hohe See, September 1914. Im Vordergrund die Bordgeschütze
der HMS *Audacious*. Offenbar gilt noch der Text des Liedes –
„Britannia rules the waves".

Une escadrille de la marine britannique fend la houle de l'Atlantique,
septembre 1914. Au premier plan apparaissent les canons de
l'HMS *Audacious*. Comme le disait la chanson, à cette époque, la
Grande-Bretagne était encore « la reine des mers ».

5. Air and sea
Zu Wasser und in der Luft
Ciel et mer

The First World War was a turning point in the history of naval warfare. For close on a hundred years the British navy had been seen by many as a global police force that patrolled the oceans, making sure that the *Pax Britannica* was rigorously enforced. In the years leading up to 1914, however, the German navy had reached near parity in size and strength. During the four long years of war the two fleets risked confrontation only once, at Jutland in 1916. Thereafter Germany relied on the submarine to rule beneath the waves.

The new player soaring high above the field of battle was the plane. The best means of observation and communication, it struck terror into the hearts of civilians and infuriated the dying breed of cavalry generals. Its supporters went perhaps a little too far in extolling its military virtues. Jan Smuts, a member of Lloyd George's War Cabinet, and Hugh Montague Trenchard (first officer commanding the Royal Flying Corps) believed that, given enough planes, total victory could be achieved without the need for fighting on the ground.

That was never proved. But, in a war short of heroes, the fighting aces of France, the United States, Germany and Britain became as famous as film stars or footballers.

Der Erste Weltkrieg war ein Wendepunkt in der Geschichte der Seekriegsführung. Fast ein Jahrhundert lang war die britische Marine von vielen als eine Art internationaler Polizei angesehen worden, die auf den Weltmeeren patrouillierte und sicherstellte, dass die Pax Britannica eingehalten wurde. In den Jahren vor 1914 hatte jedoch die deutsche Marine hinsichtlich Stärke und Umfang nahezu gleichgezogen. Während der vier langen Kriegsjahre riskierten die beiden Flotten nur einmal die direkte Konfrontation – 1916 in der Schlacht am Skagerrak. Anschließend verließ sich Deutschland auf das U-Boot und die Herrschaft unter Wasser.

Hoch über dem Schlachtfeld war das Flugzeug neu im Spiel. Als hervorragendes Mittel zur Beobachtung und Aufklärung flößte es Zivilisten Schrecken ein und erboste die aussterbende Gattung der Kavalleriegeneräle. Seine Anhänger stellten seine militärischen Tugenden vielleicht in allzu rosigem Licht dar. Jan Smuts, Mitglied von Lloyd Georges Kriegskabinett, und Hugh Montague Trenchard (der erste kommandierende Offizier des Königlichen Flugkorps) glaubten, dass mit einer ausreichenden Anzahl an Flugzeugen ein umfassender Sieg errungen werden könnte, ohne dass man einen Krieg zu Lande führen müsste.

Das wurde nie bewiesen. Aber in einem Krieg, in dem es wenige Helden gab, wurden die Kampfflieger aus Frankreich, den Vereinigten Staaten, Deutschland und Großbritannien so berühmt wie Filmstars oder Fußballspieler.

La Première Guerre mondiale constitua un tournant décisif dans l'histoire de la guerre navale. Pendant près de cent ans, la marine britannique fut considérée comme une sorte de police mondiale qui patrouillait sur les mers, s'assurant que la Pax Britannica était scrupuleusement respectée. Durant les années qui précédèrent 1914, la marine allemande devint pratiquement son égale, en taille et en force. Au cours des quatre longues années de la guerre, les deux flottes risquèrent la confrontation une fois seulement, à Jutland en 1916. À partir de là, l'Allemagne compta sur sa flotte sous-marine pour régner sous les mers.

L'avion devint ce nouveau protagoniste qui s'élevait bien au-dessus du champ de bataille. Doté de meilleurs moyens d'observation et de communication, il semait la terreur parmi les civils et enrageait les généraux de cavalerie. Les partisans de l'avion exagéraient certainement quand ils évoquaient ses vertus militaires. Jan Smuts, un membre du Cabinet de guerre de Lloyd George, et Hugh Montague Trenchard (premier officier à commander les Royal Flying Corps) estimaient que s'ils disposaient d'avions en nombre suffisant, il serait possible de remporter une victoire totale sans avoir à combattre au sol.

Cette théorie ne fut jamais prouvée. Mais, dans une guerre où les héros manquaient, les chevaliers du ciel, qu'ils soient français, américains, allemands ou britanniques, devinrent aussi connus que des stars de cinéma ou des footballeurs.

(Above) Eddie Rickenbacker at the controls of his French SPAD 13, 1917. Rickenbacker was the top US ace, with twenty-six kills. (Opposite) British SE-5s in a dogfight with German Fokker D7s, 1915.

(Oben) Eddie Rickenbacker am Steuerknüppel seiner französischen SPAD 13, 1917. Rickenbacker war mit 26 Abschüssen der Topflieger der USA. (Gegenüberliegende Seite) Britische SE-5-Maschinen in verbissenem Kampf mit deutschen Flugzeugen des Typs Fokker D7, 1915.

(Ci-dessus) Eddie Rickenbacker aux manettes de son SPAD 13 français, 1917. Rickenbacker était le meilleur pilote américain, ayant abattu 26 avions. (Ci-contre) Des SE-5 britanniques engagés dans un combat aérien contre des Fokker D7 allemands, 1915.

(Opposite) A German biplane drops a bomb, 1917.
(Right) A German balloon drops an observer, 1918.
He is parachuting to safety after the balloon has been hit.

(Gegenüberliegende Seite) Eine Bombe fällt aus einem deutschen Doppeldecker, 1917. (Rechts) Ein Beobachter springt aus einem deutschen Ballon, 1918. Er rettet sich per Fallschirm, nachdem der Ballon getroffen worden ist.

(Ci-contre) Un biplan allemand larguant une bombe, 1917. (À droite) Un observateur saute en parachute d'une montgolfière allemande qui vient d'être touchée, 1918. Il sera sauvé grâce à son parachute.

(Above) The crow's nest and foredeck of the USS *Kentucky*, January 1917. (Opposite) Sopwith 2F1 Camels on the deck of HMS *Furious*. These aircraft were flown from the carrier in July 1918 to bomb Zeppelins in their sheds at Tondern.

(Oben) Krähennest und Vorderdeck der USS *Kentucky,* Januar 1917. (Gegenüberliegende Seite) Sopwith 2F1 Camels auf dem Deck der HMS *Furious*. Diese Flugzeuge wurden im Juli 1918 vom Träger aus gestartet, um Zeppeline in ihren Hangars bei Tondern zu bombardieren.

(Ci-dessus) Le nid de pie et le pont avant du USS *Kentucky,* janvier 1917. (Ci-contre) Des Camel Sopwith 2F1 sur le pont du HMS *Furious*. Ces avions décollaient des porte-avions pour aller bombarder les Zeppelins des hangars de Tondern, juillet 1918.

The German battle-cruiser *Blücher* moments before sinking off the Dogger Bank, 24 January 1915. Seven hundred sailors were drowned.

Der deutsche Panzerkreuzer *Blücher,* kurz bevor er auf der Doggerbank am 24. Januar 1915 sank. Siebenhundert Matrosen ertranken.

Le cuirassier allemand *Blücher* quelques minutes avant de couler au large de Dogger Bank, le 24 janvier 1915. Sept cents marins moururent noyés.

Measures taken against the menace of the Zeppelin raids. (Opposite) An apron hangs from balloons as part of London's air defences, 1915. (Above) Searchlights pick up a Zeppelin during a night raid, 1916.

Maßnahmen gegen die Bedrohung durch Zeppelinangriffe. (Gegenüberliegende Seite) Eine an Ballons aufgehängte Schürze als Teil der Londoner Luftverteidigung, 1915. (Oben) Suchscheinwerfer finden einen Zeppelin während eines Nachtangriffs, 1916.

Mesures pour faire face à la menace des zeppelins. (Ci-contre) Ce 'tablier' suspendu à des ballons dans le ciel de Londres fait partie des systèmes de défense aérienne mis en place. (Ci-dessus) Zeppelin repéré par des projecteurs durant un raid nocturne, 1916.

A hand-operated siren sounds the warning of an air-raid over the
rooftops of Paris, 20 October 1917. London and Paris were the
cities to suffer most from bombing raids during the war.

Eine handbetriebene Sirene über den Dächern von Paris warnt am
20. Oktober 1917 vor einem Luftangriff. London und Paris waren die
Städte, die während des Krieges am meisten unter Bombenangriffen
zu leiden hatten.

Sirène actionnée manuellement pour signaler un raid aérien au-dessus
des toits de Paris, 20 octobre 1917. Durant cette guerre, Londres et
Paris furent les villes les plus touchées par les bombardements aériens.

Remains of a Zeppelin at Potters Bar, Hertfordshire, 2 October 1916. 'Flames shot up from the top of the Zep and there were shouts and cheers…We all rushed out. The Zeppelin was all alight, falling like some burning firey star…' – from an eyewitness account.

Überreste eines Zeppelins bei Potters Bar, Hertfordshire, 2. Oktober 1916. „Flammen schossen aus dem oberen Teil des Zeppelins empor, und es gab viel Gebrüll und Hochrufe … Wir eilten alle ins Freie. Der Zeppelin stand ganz und gar in Flammen und fiel zu Boden wie ein brennender Leuchtstern …" – aus einem Augenzeugenbericht.

Débris d'un zeppelin à Potters Bar (Hertfordshire), 2 octobre 1916. « Des flammes émergeaient du dessus du zeppelin, on entendait des cris et des exclamations. On est tous sortis précipitamment. Le zeppelin était en feu et tombait comme une météorite en flammes … » déclara un témoin de la scène.

A French aviator helps load bombs on to his biplane, 1 June 1915.
Bombers had a two-man crew. The bomber sat behind the pilot and
simply dropped bombs over the side of the plane.

Ein französischer Flieger hilft beim Verladen von Bomben in seinen
Doppeldecker, 1. Juni 1915. Bomber hatten eine Besatzung von
zwei Mann. Der Bombenschütze saß hinter dem Piloten und ließ
die Bomben einfach über die Flanke des Flugzeugs fallen.

Un aviateur français aide au chargement des bombes sur son
biplan, 1ᵉʳ juin 1915. Les bombardiers comptaient deux membres
d'équipage, le pilote et celui qui jetait les bombes par-dessus bord.

The body of a German pilot, 1916. Before the invention of the parachute, there was nothing that could be done to escape from a crippled plane. Senior officers opposed the use of the parachute, claiming it would encourage cowardice in action.

Die Leiche eines deutschen Piloten, 1916. Vor der Erfindung des Fallschirms gab es keine Möglichkeit, aus einem defekten Flugzeug zu entkommen. Führende Offiziere waren gegen den Gebrauch von Fallschirmen und behaupteten, sie würden die Feigheit vor dem Feind begünstigen.

Corps d'un pilote allemand, 1916. Jusqu'à l'invention du parachute, il n'y avait aucun moyen de survivre à un accident d'avion. Les officiers supérieurs étaient opposés à l'emploi de parachutes, affirmant que cela encouragerait les actes de lâcheté.

Baron Manfred
von Richthofen
('The Red Baron')
returns to earth after
a reconnaissance
flight in his Albatross.

Baron Manfred
von Richthofen
(der „Rote Baron")
kehrt nach einem
Aufklärungsflug in
seinem Albatros auf
festen Boden zurück.

Le baron Manfred
von Richthofen
(« le Baron Rouge »)
pose pied à terre
après un vol de
reconnaissance à
bord de son Albatros.

Von Richthofen's famous 'Flying Circus' – the 11th Pursuit Squadron – on parade in a field in France, 1917. Von Richthofen died when he was shot down over the Somme on 22 April 1918. He was credited with eighty 'kills'.

Von Richthofens berühmter „Fliegender Zirkus" – die 11. Jagdstaffel – bei einer Parade auf offenem Feld in Frankreich, 1917. Von Richthofen starb, als er am 22. April 1918 über der Somme abgeschossen wurde. Ihm wurden 80 Abschüsse zugeschrieben.

Revue du célèbre « cirque volant » de von Richthofen – la 11ᵉ escadrille de chasse – sur un champ en France, 1917. Von Richthofen mourut en vol, son avion ayant été abattu au-dessus de la Somme le 22 avril 1918. On lui attribua 80 « prises ».

American pilots in flying gear await the call to arms in their tent at
Toul, on the Moselle, 6 October 1918. An almost identical picture
could have been taken twenty-five years later.

Amerikanische Piloten in Flugmontur erwarten den Einsatzbefehl
in ihrem Zelt bei Toul an der Mosel, 6. Oktober 1918. Ein beinahe identisches Bild hätte auch 25 Jahre später aufgenommen
werden können.

Des pilotes américains en tenue de vol attendent l'appel aux armes
dans leur tente à Toul en Moselle, 6 octobre 1918. Vingt-cinq ans
plus tard, la même scène ou presque aurait pu être photographiée.

A meeting between two arms of modern technology. A US army cameraman films the take-off of an American Nieuport 28 biplane in the summer of 1918. The tented hangar indicates that aerodromes were portable affairs.

Eine Begegnung zweier Entwicklungen moderner Technik. Ein Kameramann der US-Armee filmt den Start eines amerikanischen Nieuport-28-Doppeldeckers im Sommer 1918. Der zeltartige Hangar zeigt, dass Flughafenanlagen damals transportables Gerät waren.

Rencontre entre deux armes de la technologie moderne. Un caméraman américain filme le décollage d'un biplan Nieuport 28 américain en été 1918. La tente qui sert de hangar indique que les aérodromes se montaient n'importe où.

Falling from the skies. The vertical landing of a British seaplane, 10 May 1917.
In machines made largely of wood and canvas, a pilot's chance of surviving a
crash was better over water than over land.

Vom Himmel gefallen. Die Senkrechtlandung eines britischen Seeflugzeuges
am 10. Mai 1917. Die Chancen eines Piloten, in einer Maschine, die vorwie-
gend aus Holz und Leinwand bestand, einen Absturz zu überleben, waren über
Wasser besser als über Land.

Tombé du ciel. Atterrissage vertical d'un hydravion britannique, 10 mai 1917.
Les appareils étant surtout conçus en bois et en toile, les chances de survie d'un
pilote étaient plus élevées au-dessus de l'eau que sur la terre ferme.

Steaming into action. A battleship comes under fire during the Battle of Jutland, 31 May 1916. Two hundred and fifty ships and twenty-five admirals clashed in a battle that lasted little more than ten minutes.

Mit Volldampf in den Kampf. Ein Kriegsschiff wird bei der Schlacht am Skagerrak am 31. Mai 1916 unter Beschuss genommen. Zweihundertfünfzig Schiffe und 25 Admiräle trafen in einer Schlacht aufeinander, die kaum länger als 10 Minuten dauerte.

En route pour la bataille. Un navire de guerre pénètre dans le feu de la bataille de Jutland, 31 mai 1916. 250 navires et 25 amiraux se confrontèrent durant une bataille qui ne dura guère plus de dix minutes.

One of the most feared weapons of the war – a German U-boat – surfaces, 1917.
It was the year that Germany announced unrestricted submarine warfare, an action
that provoked President Wilson into declaring the 'armed neutrality' of the USA.

Eine der meistgefürchteten Kriegswaffen – ein deutsches U-Boot – taucht auf, 1917.
Es war das Jahr, in dem Deutschland den uneingeschränkten U-Boot-Krieg ausrief,
eine Maßnahme, die Präsident Wilson zur Erklärung der „bewaffneten Neutralität"
der USA veranlasste.

Un sous-marin allemand – une des armes les plus craintes au cours de cette guerre –
fait surface, 1917. Cette année-là, l'Allemagne annonça qu'elle s'engageait dans une
guerre navale illimitée, déclaration qui conduisit le président Wilson à proclamer
« la neutralité armée » des États-Unis.

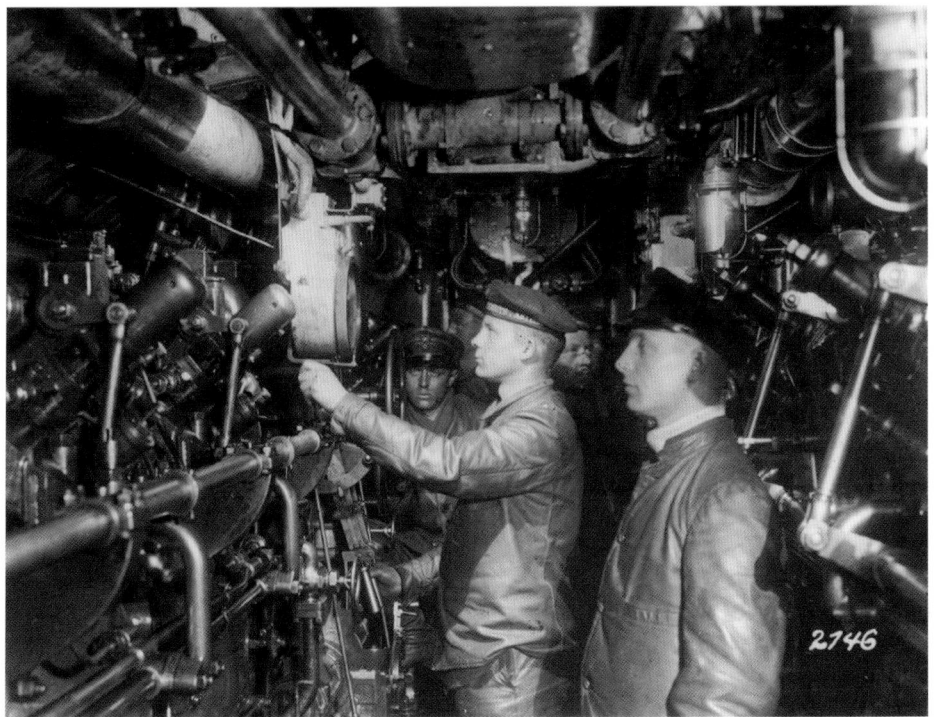

The engine room of a U-boat, 1916. Though greatly feared, U-boats inflicted far less damage than the public were led to believe by the huge publicity that was given to U-boat 'kills'.

Maschinenraum eines U-Bootes, 1916. Obwohl sie weithin gefürchtet waren, richteten U-Boote sehr viel weniger Schaden an, als in der Öffentlichkeit wegen der großen Publizität von U-Boot-Angriffen angenommen werden musste.

Salle des machines d'un sous-marin, 1916. Bien que terriblement craints, les sous-marins ne causèrent pas autant de dégâts que ce que le public imaginait sous l'influence de la très grande publicité faite aux attaques des sous-marins.

(Above) The team that built the US destroyer *Liberty* in only seventeen days poses for the camera on the day of her completion, 1917. (Opposite) A large crowd watches the launch of yet another American ship, 1918.

(Oben) Die Mannschaft, die in nur 17 Tagen den US-Zerstörer *Liberty* baute, versammelt sich am Tag der Fertigstellung vor der Kamera, 1917. (Gegenüberliegende Seite) Und wieder läuft ein amerikanisches Schiff vor den Augen einer großen Menschenmenge vom Stapel, 1918.

(Ci-dessus) L'équipe qui vient d'achever la construction du destroyer américain *Liberty* en seulement 17 jours pose pour les caméras, 1917. (Ci-contre) Une grande foule assiste au baptême d'un navire américain, encore un autre, en 1918.

6. Peace
Frieden
La paix

Cheering crowds on a London bus greet the signing of the Armistice, 11 November 1918. At last the war was over – and in time for Christmas, though four years too late to save 10 million lives.

Jubelnde Menschen auf einem Londoner Omnibus feiern die Unterzeichnung des Waffenstillstands, 11. November 1918. Endlich war der Krieg vorüber – und das vor Weihnachten, allerdings vier Jahre zu spät, um 10 Millionen Leben zu retten.

La foule enthousiaste, montée à bord d'un bus londonien, accueille dans la joie la signature de l'Armistice, le 11 novembre 1918. La guerre était enfin finie, et à temps pour fêter Noël, mais quatre ans trop tard pour sauver dix millions de vies humaines.

6. Peace
Frieden
La paix

The guns finally stopped firing at the eleventh hour of the eleventh day of the eleventh month of 1918. On the Western Front there was no fraternisation and little rejoicing, just an intense degree of relief. Many veterans noted that within half an hour of the guns falling silent the birds began to sing again.

In Paris, New York and London, the moment was greeted more raucously. Workers poured out of shops and offices. Buses were commandeered, filled with soldiers, sailors and civilians and driven through thronging crowds to the city centres. Bonfires and fireworks illuminated parks, squares and avenues. People sang and danced, waved flags, collapsed in drunken joy. The celebrations continued for three days until police gradually restored order.

In Berlin, the Armistice was greeted with almost total silence. Ten-year-old Steffie Spira went with her sister to see the ragged, worn-out, dishevelled soldiers arriving at the Brandenburg Gate. 'It was a sad occasion – people cried… I gave a soldier my little bouquet and he said "Good luck to you, little miss." I will never forget the grief in his eyes.'

In der elften Stunde des elften Tages des elften Monats des Jahres 1918 wurde schließlich das Feuer eingestellt. An der Westfront gab es keine Verbrüderungsszenen und wenig Frohlocken, nur ein intensives Gefühl der Erleichterung. Viele Heimkehrer bemerkten, dass kaum eine halbe Stunde nach dem Schweigen der Waffen die Vögel begannen, wieder zu singen.

In Paris, New York und London wurde der Anlass stürmischer gefeiert. Arbeiter strömten aus Läden und Büros. Busse wurden gekapert, mit Soldaten, Matrosen und Zivilisten gefüllt und durch dichte Menschenmassen ins Zentrum der Städte manövriert.

Freudenfeuer und Feuerwerke erleuchteten Parks, Plätze und Avenuen. Die Menschen sangen und tanzten, schwenkten Flaggen, brachen freudetrunken zusammen. Die Feiern hielten drei Tage lang an, bis die Polizeikräfte nach und nach die Ordnung wiederherstellten.

In Berlin begegnete man dem Waffenstillstand mit einem fast vollständigen Schweigen. Die 10 Jahre alte Steffie Spira begleitete ihre Schwester, um die Ankunft der zerlumpten, ausgemergelten, verwahrlosten Soldaten am Brandenburger Tor zu sehen. „Es war ein trauriger Tag – die Menschen weinten … Ich schenkte einem Soldaten meinen kleinen Blumenstrauß, und er sagte: ‚Viel Glück, kleines Fräulein.' Niemals werde ich den Schmerz in seinen Augen vergessen."

Les canons se turent enfin à onze heures du matin le onzième jour du onzième mois de l'année 1918. Sur le front Ouest, il n'y eut aucune scène de fraternisation, à peine quelques signes de joie, simplement un énorme sentiment de soulagement. Nombre de vétérans notèrent qu'une demi-heure après que le silence des armes se fit, les oiseaux chantèrent à nouveau.

À Paris, à New York et à Londres, l'événement fut fêté plus bruyamment. Les employés sortirent en masse des magasins et bureaux. Les bus furent réquisitionnés, remplis de soldats, de marins et de civils puis conduits à travers une foule grouillante vers le centre ville. Des feux de joie et des feux d'artifice illuminèrent les parcs, les places et les avenues. Les gens chantèrent et dansèrent, agitèrent des drapeaux, tombèrent ivres de joie. Les célébrations se poursuivirent pendant trois jours avant que la police ne restaure l'ordre progressivement.

À Berlin, l'armistice fut accueillie dans un silence quasi total. La petite Steffie Spira, âgée de 10 ans, et sa sœur assistèrent au retour des soldats en lambeaux, hirsutes et épuisés par la Porte de Brandenbourg. « C'était triste … les gens pleuraient … J'ai donné mon petit bouquet de fleurs à un soldat et il m'a dit ‹ bonne chance, ma petite demoiselle ›. Je n'oublierai jamais la tristesse de son regard. »

(Above) Anticipating the event. On 4 October 1918, the crew of the *Victory* parade to spell out the name of their ship and their goal. (Opposite) At Camp Sherman, Ohio, 21,000 officers and soldiers form the head of President Wilson, 1918.

(Oben) Vorgegriffen. Am 4. Oktober 1918 stellt die Besatzung der *Victory* bei einer Parade nicht nur den Namen ihres Schiffes dar, sondern auch ihr Ziel, den „Sieg". (Gegenüberliegende Seite) Im Camp Sherman, Ohio, formen 21 000 Offiziere und Soldaten den Kopf von Präsident Wilson, 1918.

(Ci-dessus) Anticipation. Le 4 octobre 1918, l'équipage du *Victory* défile en formant les lettres de leur navire et de leur objectif. (Ci-contre) À Camp Sherman (Ohio), 21 000 officiers et soldats s'unirent pour former la tête du Président Wilson, 1918.

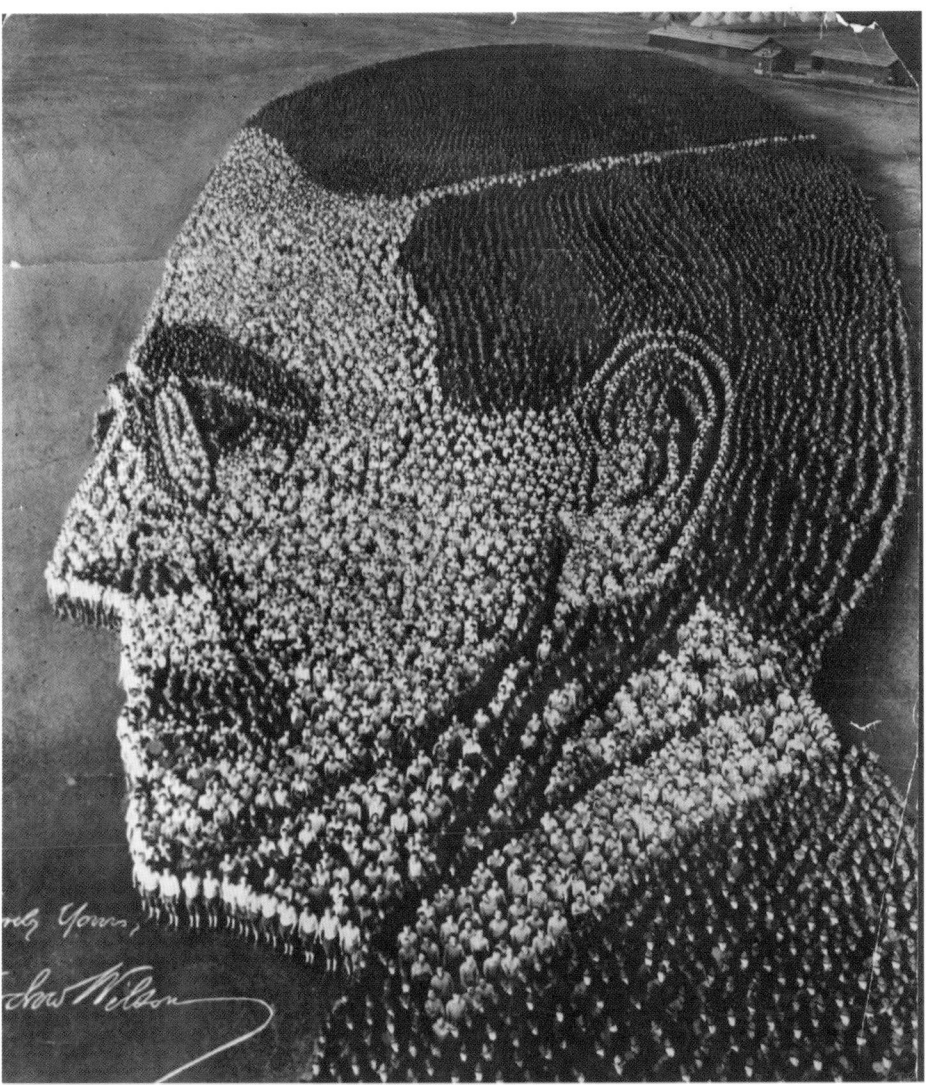

Tens of thousands of Londoners gather in Trafalgar Square to celebrate the signing of the Peace Treaty at Versailles, June 1919. The War to End All Wars was finally and irrevocably over.

Zehntausende versammeln sich auf dem Londoner Trafalgar Square, um die Unterzeichnung des Friedensvertrages in Versailles im Juni 1919 zu feiern. Der „Krieg, der das Ende aller Kriege bedeutete", war endlich und unwiderruflich vorüber.

Des dizaines de milliers de Londoniens se rassemblèrent à Trafalgar Square pour célébrer la signature du Traité de paix de Versailles, juin 1919. La Grande Guerre, celle qui devait mettre fin à toutes les guerres, était définitivement et irrévocablement finie.

Happy and affluent. One of the tables of merrymakers at the Ritz Hotel, London, November 1918. At the Savoy, according to Noël Coward: 'Everybody wore paper caps, and threw streamers, and drank champagne and sang the *Marseillaise*…'

Glück und Wohlstand. Eine fröhliche Tafelrunde, die im November 1918 im Ritz, London, feiert. So ging es auch im Savoy zu, wie Noël Coward berichtet: „Alle Welt trug Papierhüte, warf mit bunten Schlangen und trank Champagner und sang die Marseillaise …"

Heureux et riches. Une table de joyeux convives au Ritz Hotel à Londres, novembre 1918. Au Savoy, selon Noël Coward « tout le monde portait des chapeaux en papier, jetait des serpentins, buvait du champagne et chantait La Marseillaise … »

Street of sorrow – Berlin in the immediate post-war period. People who had spent the last three years surviving on less than 1,000 calories a day now faced hunger, poverty, squalor and revolution.

Straße des Leidens – Berlin unmittelbar nach dem Krieg. Menschen, die die letzten drei Jahre damit verbracht hatten, mit weniger als 1000 Kalorien am Tag durchzukommen, mussten jetzt gegen Hunger, Armut, Verwahrlosung und eine Revolution kämpfen.

Rue emplie de tristesse – Berlin dans l'immédiat après-guerre. Après avoir survécu trois ans à un régime quotidien de moins de 1000 calories, les gens devaient maintenant faire face à la famine, la pauvreté, des conditions de vie sordides et la révolution.

Street of joy – the East End of London at much the same time. 'Victory' parties were organised everywhere in the spring and summer of 1919 to celebrate the triumph of life over death.

Straße des Vergnügens – das Londoner East End in denselben Tagen. „Siegespartys" wurden im Frühling und Sommer 1919 überall organisiert, um den Triumph des Lebens über den Tod zu feiern.

Rue emplie de gaieté – l'East End de Londres à la même époque ou presque. Des fêtes de la « victoire » furent organisées partout durant le printemps et l'été 1919 pour célébrer le triomphe de la vie sur la mort.

The caricature Kaiser. A crowd of revellers celebrates the Armistice in London,
11 November 1918. The caption to the drawing reads: 'Gone to a better [h]ole',
a reference to a famous First World War cartoon by Bruce Bairnsfather.

Karikierter Kaiser. Eine frohlockende Menge feiert den Waffenstillstand in London
am 11. November 1918. Die Plakatunterschrift lautet: „Gone to a better [h]ole",
eine Anspielung auf eine berühmte Kriegskarikatur von Bruce Bairnsfather.

Caricature de l'Empereur. Une bande de fêtards célébrant l'Armistice à Londres,
le 11 novembre 1918. La légende du dessin dit : « Parti se cacher dans un meilleur
trou », en référence à un célèbre dessin humoristique de Bruce Bairnsfather durant
la Première Guerre mondiale.

The real Kaiser. His Imperial Highness the Emperor Wilhelm II of Germany in the gardens of his home in the Netherlands following his abdication and exile, 28 December 1918. A month earlier he had exclaimed: 'It's just that damned Berlin that's against me!'

Wirklicher Kaiser. Seine Kaiserliche Hoheit Wilhelm II. von Deutschland im Park seines Refugiums in den Niederlanden am 28. November 1918, nachdem er abgedankt hatte und ins Exil gegangen war. Noch einen Monat zuvor hatte er ausgerufen: „Nur dieses verdammte Berlin ist gegen mich!"

Le vrai empereur. Son Altesse impériale l'empereur Guillaume II d'Allemagne dans les jardins de sa demeure aux Pays-Bas où il s'est exilé après avoir abdiqué le 28 décembre 1918. Un mois plus tôt il s'était écrié « ce n'est que ce fichu Berlin qui est contre moi ! ».

The German delegates arrive at the Versailles Peace Conference, led by the Foreign Minister, Ulrich Graf von Brockdorff-Rantzau, 7 May 1919. It was the day that the Peace Treaty was first handed to the Germans.

Die deutsche Delegation trifft zur Friedenskonferenz in Versailles ein, angeführt von Außenminister Ulrich Graf von Brockdorff-Rantzau, 7. Mai 1919. Es war der Tag, an dem die Deutschen den Friedensvertrag erstmals zu sehen bekamen.

Arrivée à la Conférence de paix à Versailles des délégués allemands, avec à leur tête le ministre des Affaires étrangères, Ulrich Graf von Brockdorff-Rantzau, le 7 mai 1919. Ce fut ce jour-là que les Allemands prirent connaissance du Traité de paix pour la première fois.

The Allied triumvirate arrives at Versailles, 1 June 1919 – (from left to right) Georges Clémenceau, Prime Minister of France; Woodrow Wilson, President of the USA; and Lloyd George, the British Prime Minister.

Das Alliierte Triumvirat trifft am 1. Juni 1919 in Versailles ein – Georges Clémenceau, französischer Premierminister, Woodrow Wilson, Präsident der USA, und Lloyd George, der britische Premierminister (von links nach rechts).

Le triumvirat des Alliés à son arrivée à Versailles, le 1er juin 1919 – (de gauche à droite) Georges Clémenceau, le Premier ministre français, Woodrow Wilson, le président des États-Unis, et Lloyd George, le Premier ministre britannique.

Allied officers peer through the windows into the
Hall of Mirrors to witness the signing of the Peace Treaty,
28 June 1919. The German delegation had no choice. Had
they refused to sign, Germany would have been invaded.

Alliierte Offizierc, die durch die Fenster in den Spiegelsaal
spähen, werden Zeuge der Unterzeichnung des Friedensvertrages am 28. Juni 1919. Der deutschen Delegation
blieb keine Wahl. Eine Verweigerung der Unterschrift hätte
die Invasion Deutschlands bedeutet.

Les officiers alliés assistent, en regardant à travers les
fenêtres de la Salle des glaces, à la signature du Traité de
paix, le 28 juin 1919. La délégation allemande n'eut
aucun choix. Si elle avait refusé de signer, l'Allemagne
aurait été envahie.

A member of the German air force cuts up a pile of airmen's helmets, 1919. Under the terms of the Treaty of Versailles, Germany was compelled to destroy almost all military weapons and equipment.

Ein Angehöriger der deutschen Luftwaffe zerschneidet 1919 einen Haufen Fliegerhelme. Nach den Bedingungen des Versailler Vertrages war Deutschland gezwungen, fast alle militärischen Waffen und Ausrüstungsgegenstände zu zerstören.

Un soldat de l'armée de l'air allemande découpe des casques de pilote à la chaîne, 1919. Selon les termes du Traité de Versailles, l'Allemagne était obligée de détruire la quasi-totalité de son armement et de son équipement militaire.

A tank is dismembered on the outskirts of Berlin, 1919. Although the machine bears the German insignia, it was in fact a British tank, captured on the Western Front late in the war.

In den Außenbezirken Berlins wird 1919 ein Panzer zerlegt. Obwohl das Fahrzeug die deutschen Hoheitszeichen trägt, handelt es sich um einen britischen Panzer, der gegen Ende des Krieges erbeutet wurde.

Démembrement d'un char dans les environs de Berlin, 1919. Bien que cet engin porte l'insigne allemand, il s'agit en fait d'un char britannique, saisi sur le front Ouest vers la fin de la guerre.

The German High Seas Fleet surrenders to Admiral Beatty in the cold waters of
Scapa Flow in the Orkney Islands, Scotland, 21 November 1918. It had never
before been defeated in battle.

Die deutsche Hochseeflotte ergibt sich Admiral Beatty in den kalten Gewässern
von Scapa Flow bei den Orkneyinseln, Schottland, 21. November 1918. Sie war
nie zuvor im Kampf besiegt worden.

La flotte allemande des hautes mers se rend à l'Amiral Beatty dans les eaux froides
de Scapa Flow dans les îles Orkney (Écosse), le 21 novembre 1918. Elle était restée
invaincue jusque-là.

Viscount Curzon, a member of Lloyd George's War Cabinet, films the surrender of the German fleet at Scapa Flow. Seven months later, the ships were scuttled by their crews, in protest against the terms of the Treaty of Versailles.

Graf Curzon, ein Mitglied des Kriegskabinetts von Lloyd George, filmt die Kapitulation der deutschen Flotte bei Scapa Flow. Sieben Monate später wurden die Schiffe aus Protest gegen die Bedingungen des Versailler Vertrages von ihren Mannschaften versenkt.

Le vicomte Curzon, un membre du cabinet de guerre de Lloyd George, filme la reddition de la flotte allemande à Scapa Flow. Sept mois plus tard, les navires furent sabordés par les équipages pour protester contre les termes du Traité de Versailles.

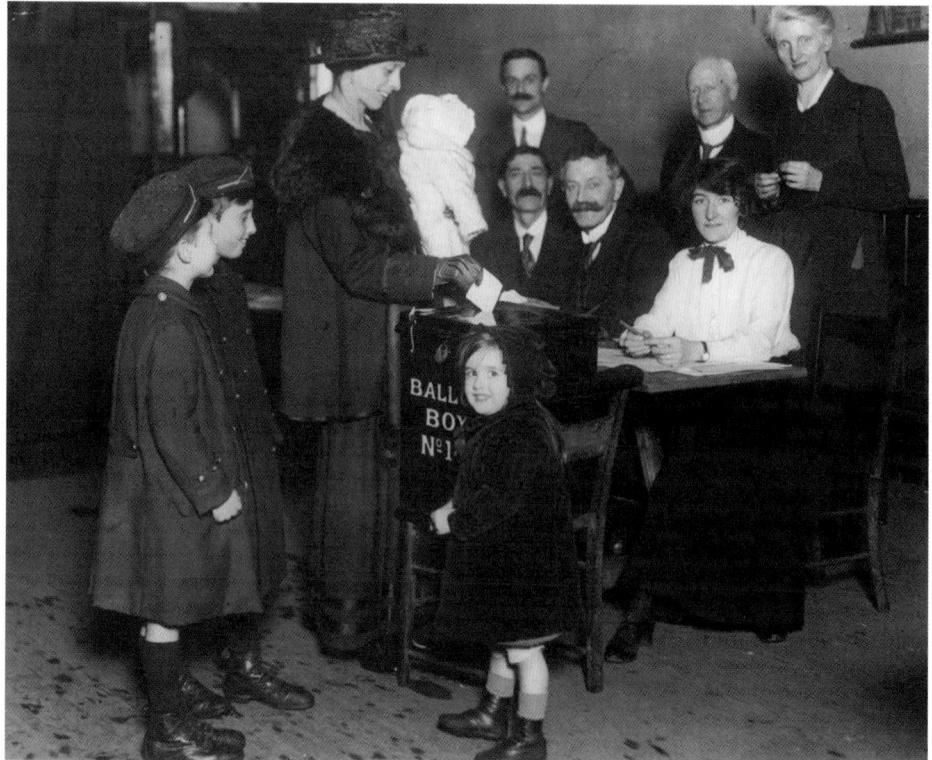

One of the fruits of victory – a newly-enfranchised woman votes for the first time in a British Parliamentary election, 14 December 1918. Women over 30 years of age had been given the vote.

Eine der Früchte des Sieges – eine erstmals wahlberechtigte Frau nimmt an der Wahl zum britischen Parlament teil. Frauen über 30 hatten das Wahlrecht erhalten.

Un des fruits de la victoire – Cette femme vote pour la première fois à l'occasion d'élections pour le Parlement britannique, le 14 décembre 1918. Le droit de vote avait été accordé aux femmes âgées de plus de 30 ans.

Nancy Witcher Langhorne, Viscountess Astor, with her husband William Waldorf Astor, campaigns for the Conservative Party in Plymouth during the 1919 election. Although born in the United States, she became the first woman MP in Britain.

Nancy Witcher Langhorne, Gräfin Astor, mit ihrem Ehemann William Waldorf Astor, im Wahlkampf für die Konservative Partei in Plymouth, 1919. Obwohl in den Vereinigten Staaten geboren, wurde sie die erste weibliche Parlamentsabgeordnete in Großbritannien.

La vicomtesse Astor, Nancy Witcher Langhorne, accompagnée de son mari William Waldorf Astor, fait campagne pour le parti conservateur à Plymouth lors de l'élection de 1919. Bien que née aux États-Unis, elle fut la première femme élue députée au Parlement britannique.

7. Revolution
Revolution
La Révolution

'We shall now proceed to construct the socialist order…'
Vladimir Ilyich Lenin addresses a crowd, 1917. Lenin was the
architect, midwife and guiding spirit of the Bolshevik Revolution.

„Als Nächstes werden wir jetzt die sozialistische Ordnung
aufbauen …" Wladimir Iljitsch Lenin als Redner vor der Menge,
1917. Lenin war der Architekt, die Hebamme und der leitende
Geist der bolschewistischen Revolution.

« Nous allons maintenant instaurer l'ordre socialiste … » déclare
Vladimir Illich Lénine à la foule, 1917. Lénine fut l'architecte,
l'accoucheur et le guide spirituel de la Révolution bolchevique.

7. Revolution
Revolution
La Révolution

In the restless years from 1910 to 1919 revolution raised its spitting, snarling head all over the world. There were revolutions and rebellions in Nicaragua and Mexico. Portugal erupted in violence in October 1910, forcing King Manuel II to make his way hastily to Gibraltar. Ulster spluttered and threatened civil war in 1913. Dublin broke out in armed insurrection three years later. The vicissitudes of war proved too much for the peoples of the old empires of Europe. In October 1918 the Austro-Hungarian Empire disintegrated.

Within the next few months there were revolutions in Germany and Hungary. Berlin was the centre of German discontent. Democrats, Communists, and members of the *Freikorps* clashed on the streets. Horrendous killings took place against a background of poverty, starvation and economic depression.

But the most shattering of all was the Russian Revolution. Imperial Russia was overthrown by a crescendo of risings and protests that culminated in the Bolshevik coup of November 1917. The Tsar and his family, whose public glory had been matched by their private sadness, were taken by Red Guards to Yekaterinburg, where they were shot in July 1918. The rule of the Romanovs had come to a bitter and bloody end.

In den unruhigen Jahren zwischen 1910 und 1919 erhob die Revolution überall in der Welt ihr Gift speiendes, knurrendes Haupt. Revolutionen und Rebellionen gab es in Nicaragua und Mexiko. In Portugal brach die Gewalt im Oktober 1910 aus und zwang König Manuel II. zur Flucht nach Gibraltar. Ulster kochte 1913 über, der Bürgerkrieg drohte. In Dublin brachen bewaffnete Aufstände drei Jahre später aus. Für die Völker der alten Reiche Europas waren die Wechselfälle des Krieges mehr, als sie ertragen konnten. Österreich-Ungarn zerfiel im Oktober 1918.

Innerhalb der nächsten paar Monate gab es Revolutionen in Deutschland und Ungarn. Berlin wurde zum Zentrum der deutschen Unzufriedenheit. Demokraten, Kommunisten und Mitglieder der Freikorps lieferten einander Straßenkämpfe. Vor einem Hintergrund von Armut, drohendem Verhungern und wirtschaftlicher Depression fanden schreckliche Massaker statt.

Die gewaltigste von allen aber war die Russische Revolution. Das kaiserliche Russland wurde in ein Crescendo von Aufständen und Protesten gestürzt, die im bolschewistischen Staatsstreich vom November 1917 gipfelten. Der Zar und seine Familie, die öffentlichen Ruhm und Glanz in gleichem Maße erfuhren wie privates Unglück, wurde von den Roten Garden nach Jekaterinburg gebracht und dort im Juli 1918 erschossen. Die Herrschaft der Romanows hatte ihr bitteres und blutiges Ende gefunden.

Durant les années agitées de 1910 à 1919, le visage grondant et explosif de la révolution se dressa partout dans le monde. Il y eut des soulèvements et des rebellions au Nicaragua et au Mexique. Le Portugal sombra dans la violence en octobre 1910, obligeant le roi Manuel II à s'enfuir à Gibraltar. En Ulster, le climat devint explosif et, en 1913, la guerre civile menaçait. Trois ans plus tard, Dublin se souleva et sombra dans l'insurrection armée. Les vicissitudes de la guerre se révélèrent insurmontables pour les peuples des vieux empires de l'Europe et, en octobre 1918, l'Empire austro-hongrois se désintégra.

Dans les mois qui suivirent, la révolution éclata en Allemagne et en Hongrie. Berlin fut le centre du mécontentement allemand. Les démocrates, les communistes et les membres des *Freikorps* se bagarraient dans la rue. Des tueries horribles eurent lieu sur fond de pauvreté, de famine et de crise économique.

Mais la révolution russe fut la plus bouleversante de toutes. La Russie impériale fut renversée suite à une série de soulèvements et de manifestations qui culminèrent avec le coup d'état bolchevique de novembre 1917. Le Tsar et sa famille, dont la gloire publique n'avait d'égal que leur tristesse en privé, furent emmenés par la garde Rouge à Yekaterinbourg et exécutés en juillet 1918. Le règne des Romanov prit fin dans le sang et l'amertume.

The Big Three of the
Revolution. (Left to
right) Joseph Stalin,
Lenin and Mikhail
Ivanovich Kalinin at
the Congress of the
Russian Communist
Party, March 1919.

Die Großen Drei der
Revolution: Josef
Stalin, Lenin und
Michail Iwanowitsch
Kalinin (von links
nach rechts) beim
Parteitag der Kom-
munistischen
Partei Russlands
im März 1919.

Les trois grands
hommes de la
Révolution.
(De gauche à droite)
Joseph Staline,
Lénine et Mikhaïl
Ivanovitch Kalinine
au Congrès du Parti
Communiste russe,
mars 1919.

The siege of the Duma, July 1917. Crowds flee as fighting erupts between Bolsheviks and supporters of Alexander Kerensky's provisional government in the Nevsky Prospect, Petrograd (St Petersburg).

Die Belagerung der Duma, Juli 1917. Menschen fliehen, als auf dem Newski-Prospekt in Petrograd (St. Petersburg) zwischen Bolschewiken und Anhängern der provisorischen Regierung Alexander Kerenskis der offene Kampf ausbricht.

Le siège de la Douma, juillet 1917. La foule s'enfuit alors que des affrontements éclatent sur Nevsky Prospect à Petrograd (Saint-Pétersbourg) entre bolcheviques et partisans du gouvernement provisoire d'Alexander Kerensky.

Marines and members of the Red Guard prepare to attack the Winter Palace in Petrograd, October 1917. 'This is only a preliminary step toward a similar revolution everywhere' – Lenin.

Marinesoldaten und Mitglieder der Roten Garde bereiten sich auf die Erstürmung des Winterpalais in Petrograd vor, Oktober 1917. „Dies ist nur ein vorbereitender Schritt zu einer ähnlichen Revolution überall" – Lenin.

Les marins et membres de la garde Rouge se préparent à attaquer le palais d'Hiver à Petrograd, octobre 1917. « Ce n'est que la première étape d'une révolution qui sera similaire partout ailleurs » – Lénine.

Demonstrators outside the Winter Palace in Petrograd, 1917. Kerensky fled to Moscow. The days of the 'moderates' were numbered.

Demonstranten vor dem Winterpalais in Petrograd, 1917. Kerenski floh nach Moskau. Die Tage der „Gemäßigten" waren gezählt.

Manifestants devant le palais d'Hiver à Petrograd, 1917. Kerensky s'enfuit à Moscou. Les jours des « modérés » étaient comptés.

'Where force is necessary, one should make use of it boldly.' Leon Trotsky, newly-appointed Commissar for Foreign Affairs, watches Bolshevik troops parade in Red Square, Moscow, 1918.

„Wo Gewalt am Platze ist, sollte man sie kühn einsetzen." Leo Trotzki, frisch ernannter Kommissar für Äußere Angelegenheiten, sieht einer bolschewistischen Truppenparade auf dem Roten Platz in Moskau zu, 1918.

« Quand le recours à la force est nécessaire, il faut l'utiliser avec courage ». Léon Trotsky, le commissaire aux Affaires étrangères fraîchement nommé, assiste au défilé des troupes bolcheviques sur la place Rouge, Moscou, 1918.

A year earlier and a thousand miles to the west – Alexander Kerensky, Minister of War and leader of the provisional government, reviews Russian troops leaving for the Eastern Front, 1917.

Ein Jahr zuvor und 1500 Kilometer weiter westlich – Alexander Kerenski, Kriegsminister und Führer der provisorischen Regierung, verabschiedet russische Truppen an die Ostfront, 1917.

Un an plus tôt et à quelques milliers de kilomètres à l'Ouest, Alexandre Kerensky, ministre de la Guerre et dirigeant du gouvernement provisoire, passe en revue les troupes russes prêtes à partir pour le front Est, 1917.

(Above) Red Guards on the eve of the Bolshevik Revolution, October 1917.
(Opposite) Members of the Russian royal family on the roof of the conservatory
at Tobolsk, 1918 – (left to right) the Grand Duchesses Olga and Anastasia, the
Tsar and Tsarevich, and the Grand Duchesses Tatiana and Marie.

(Oben) Rote Garden am Vorabend der bolschewistischen Revolution, Oktober 1917.
(Gegenüberliegende Seite) Mitglieder der Zarenfamilie auf dem Dach des Konser-
vatoriums von Tobolsk, 1918 – die Großherzoginnen Olga und Anastasia, der Zar
und der Zarewitsch, die Großherzoginnen Tatjana und Marie.

(Ci-dessus) Soldats de la garde Rouge à la veille de la révolution bolchevique,
octobre 1917. (Ci-contre) Des membres de la famille royale russe sur le toit du
conservatoire à Tobolsk, 1918. (De gauche à droite) Les grandes-duchesses Olga et
Anastasia, le tsar et le tsarévitch ainsi que les grandes-duchesses Tatiana et Marie.

Daughters of the Tsar. (From left to right) The Grand Duchesses Marie, Tatiana, Anastasia and Olga in the happier days of 1914. All of them lost their lives at Yekaterinburg.

Töchter des Zaren. Die Großherzoginnen Marie, Tatjana, Anastasia und Olga (von links nach rechts) in den glücklicheren Tagen von 1914. Sie alle fanden in Jekaterinburg den Tod.

Les filles du tsar. (De gauche à droite) Les grandes-duchesses Marie, Tatiana, Anastasia et Olga au temps des jours heureux de 1914. Toutes furent exécutées à Yekaterinbourg.

Daughters of the Revolution. Female Russian soldiers, 11 August 1917. Although originally recruited to fight alongside male troops in the Tsar's army, many brigades of women soldiers fought for the Bolshevik Revolution.

Töchter der Revolution. Russische Soldatinnen am 11. August 1917. Obwohl sie ursprünglich rekrutiert worden waren, um neben männlichen Truppen für den Zaren zu kämpfen, kämpften viele Frauenbrigaden für die bolschewistische Revolution.

Filles de la Révolution et soldats russes, 11 août 1917. Initialement recrutées pour combattre aux côtés des soldats de l'armée du tsar, les brigades de femmes soldats furent nombreuses à prendre le parti de la Révolution bolchevique.

Crowds run for safety as fighting breaks out in the Nevsky Prospect, Petrograd, October 1917. 'It remains to be seen whether Petrograd will be followed by the rest of Russia' wrote Arthur Ransome, Foreign Correspondent of the *Daily News*. It was.

Menschenmengen bringen sich in Sicherheit, als auf dem Newski-Prospekt in Petrograd im Oktober 1917 die Kämpfe ausbrechen. „Es wird sich zeigen, ob das übrige Russland dem Beispiel Petrograds folgt", schrieb Arthur Ransome, Auslandskorrespondent der *Daily News*. Es zeigte sich.

La foule se disperse en courant pour échapper aux tirs sur Nevsky Prospekt à Petrograd, octobre 1917. « Est-ce que le reste de la Russie suivra l'exemple de Petrograd ? » écrivit Arthur Ransome, correspondant étranger pour le *Daily News*. C'est ce qui se passa.

Fighting on the streets of Berlin between government troops of Friedrich Ebert and the Spartacists, 1919. The Spartacists were mainly armed Communists and their supporters striving for a Socialist order.

Straßenkämpfe in Berlin zwischen den Regierungstruppen Friedrich Eberts und den Spartakisten, 1919. Bei den Spartakisten handelte es sich zumeist um bewaffnete Kommunisten, die eine sozialistische Ordnung anstrebten.

Affrontements dans les rues de Berlin entre les soldats gouvernementaux de Friedrich Ebert et les spartakistes, 1919. La plupart des spartakistes étaient la branche armée des communistes et de leurs partisans qui cherchaient à établir un ordre socialiste.

On 4 January 1919, Spartacists closed down Berlin's factories, power stations and public transport. They also occupied and raided most newspaper offices. (Above) Spartacists burn pamphlets and papers.

Am 4. Januar 1919 legten Spartakisten die Berliner Fabriken, Kraftwerke und Verkehrsbetriebe still. Sie besetzten und plünderten auch die meisten Zeitungsredaktionen. (Oben) Spartakisten verbrennen Pamphlete und Zeitungen.

Le 4 janvier 1919, les spartakistes fermèrent les usines, les centrales électriques et les transports publics de Berlin. Ils occupèrent et mirent à sac la plupart des rédactions de journaux. (Ci-dessus) Des spartakistes brûlant des pamphlets et des tracts.

The Red Flag is carried through Berlin streets, December 1918. Troops joined the Spartacists when rumours spread of a right-wing counter-revolution. The rising lasted barely two months.

Die Rote Fahne wird im Dezember 1918 durch die Berliner Straßen gefahren. Truppen schlossen sich den Spartakisten an, als sich das Gerücht einer rechtsgerichteten Gegen-revolution verbreitete. Der Aufstand hielt sich keine zwei Monate.

Le drapeau rouge est montré dans les rues de Berlin, décembre 1918. Les soldats se rangèrent aux côtés des spartakistes après la propagation de rumeurs concernant une contre-révolution de droite. Le soulèvement dura à peine deux mois.

Rosa Luxemburg, the Polish-born co-founder of the Spartacist movement, 15 January 1919. It was the day of her arrest by counter-revolutionary volunteers. Hours later she was brutally murdered by them 'while attempting to escape'.

Rosa Luxemburg, die in Polen geborene Mitbegründerin der Spartakisten-bewegung, am 15. Januar 1919. Es war der Tag ihrer Verhaftung durch Freikorps. Stunden später wurde sie „bei einem Flucht-versuch" brutal von ihnen ermordet.

Rosa Luxemburg, co-fondatrice du mouve-ment spartakiste, d'origine polonaise, photographiée le 15 janvier 1919, jour de son arresta-tion par des corps francs. Quelques heures plus tard, ces derniers l'ont sauvagement assassi-née « alors qu'elle tentait de s'enfuir ».

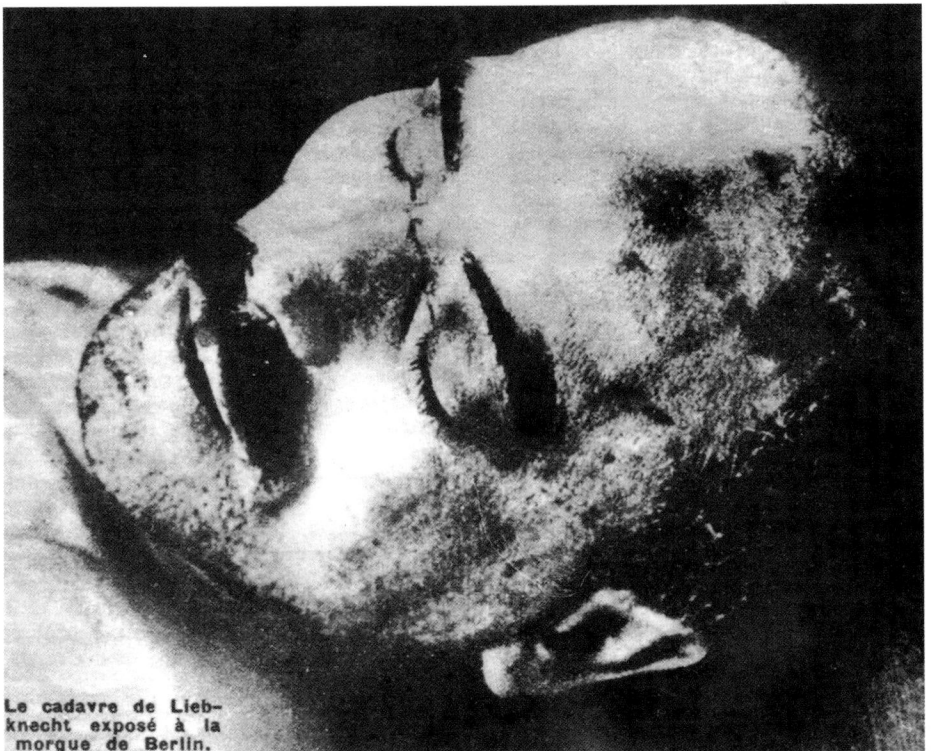

Le cadavre de Lieb-
knecht exposé à la
morgue de Berlin.

The corpse of Karl Liebknecht, co-founder of the Spartacists and leader of the party, 15 January 1919. The car carrying Liebknecht to Moabit Prison pulled up at the side of a dark road. Liebknecht was shot.

Die Leiche von Karl Liebknecht, Mitbegründer der Spartakisten und Parteiführer, 15. Januar 1919. Der Wagen, der Liebknecht ins Gefängnis Moabit überführen sollte, fuhr in einer dunklen Straße an den Bordstein. Liebknecht wurde erschossen.

Le corps de Karl Liebknecht, cofondateur et dirigeant du parti spartakiste, le 15 janvier 1919. La voiture transportant Liebknecht à la prison de Moabit s'arrêta sur le côté d'une rue peu éclairée. Liebknecht fut tué par balles.

8. Work
Arbeit
Le travail

At the height of the war, women employees of the London and North West Railway practise their skills in a typewriting class, December 1917. The smiles to the camera were almost certainly genuine.

Auf dem Höhepunkt des Krieges üben weibliche Angestellte der Eisenbahngesellschaft London and North West Railway ihre Fertigkeiten an der Schreibmaschine während einer Fortbildungsmaßnahme im Dezember 1917. Das Lächeln in die Kamera ist mit ziemlicher Sicherheit nicht gestellt.

Au plus fort de la guerre, des employées des Chemins de Fer de Londres et du Nord-Ouest s'exercent à taper à la machine lors d'une leçon de dactylographie, décembre 1917. Les sourires affichés sont probablement sincères.

8. Work
Arbeit
Le travail

Industrially, it should have been the best of times. Order books were full for coal, steel, textiles, ships and armaments. New industries were expanding; indeed, the demand for motor cars seemed inexhaustible. Wages had never been higher. In January 1914, Henry Ford offered his workers $5 a day and (except for women) a profit-sharing scheme. In 1912 the *Code du Travail* was issued in France, standardising hours and wages. In the USA, the federal government moved towards establishing an eight-hour working day.

But the workplace became increasingly a place of strife, turmoil and tragedy. Britain was hit by a series of bitter disputes involving miners, dockers and railwaymen. In America, the IWW backed strikes by textile workers in Lawrence, Massachusetts, in 1912, and four years later more than three hundred IWW members were gaoled following a miners' strike at Scranton, Pennsylvania.

Women experienced the greatest changes at work. In the war they drove buses, delivered coal, ran sections of the railway systems, became police officers, soldiers, sailors and farm-workers. For millions of women such jobs were more exciting, more enjoyable and more profitable than anything that had gone before.

Aus unternehmerischer Sicht hätten die Zeiten gar nicht besser sein können. Die Auftragsbücher für Kohle, Stahl, Textilien, Schiffe und Rüstungsgüter waren gefüllt. Neue Industriezweige expandierten; die Nachfrage nach Kraftwagen schien geradezu unstillbar. Die Löhne waren niemals höher gewesen. Im Januar 1914 bot Henry Ford seinen Arbeitern fünf Dollar am Tag und (außer den Frauen) einen Gewinnbeteiligungsplan. Der 1912 in Frankreich verabschiedete Code du travail regelte und standardisierte Arbeitszeiten und Löhne. In den USA steuerte die Regierung auf die allgemeine Einführung des Acht-Stunden-Tages zu.

Aber der Arbeitsplatz wurde zunehmend ein Ort des Kampfes, des Aufruhrs und der Tragödien. Großbritannien erlitt eine Reihe bitterer Auseinandersetzungen, an denen Bergleute, Hafenarbeiter und Eisenbahner beteiligt waren. In Amerika unterstützte die IWW (Industrial Workers of the World) 1912 Streiks von Textilarbeitern in Lawrence, Massachusetts, und vier Jahre später wurden mehr als 300 IWW-Mitglieder nach einem Bergarbeiterstreik in Scranton, Pennsylvania, ins Gefängnis geworfen.

Frauen erlebten die gravierendsten Veränderungen ihrer Arbeitswelt. Während des Krieges fuhren sie Busse, lieferten Kohle aus, leiteten Teile der Schienenbetriebe, wurden Polizistinnen, Soldatinnen, Matrosinnen und Landarbeiterinnen. Für Millionen von Frauen waren solche Arbeiten aufregender, angenehmer und Gewinn bringender als alles zuvor.

L'époque aurait dû être, dans le domaine de l'industrie, la plus formidable de toutes. Les carnets de commande étaient pleins, que ce soit pour le charbon, l'acier, le textile, les navires ou l'armement. De nouvelles industries se développaient tandis que le marché de l'automobile semblait inépuisable. Les salaires n'avaient jamais été aussi élevés. En janvier 1914, Henry Ford offrit à ses ouvriers un salaire quotidien de 5 $ ainsi qu'un plan d'intéressement aux bénéfices (mais non accessible aux femmes). En 1912, le Code du travail fut publié en France afin d'harmoniser les salaires et les heures de travail. Aux États-Unis, le gouvernement fédéral était sur le point de ratifier la journée de huit heures.

Toutefois, le monde du travail devint de plus en plus le théâtre de lutte et de tragédie. La Grande-Bretagne fut touchée par une série de conflits impliquant des mineurs, des dockers et des cheminots. Aux États-Unis, en 1912, le syndicat IWW soutint les grèves des ouvriers du textile à Lawrence, mais quatre ans plus tard, en 1918, plus de 300 membres du IWW furent emprisonnés suite à une grève de mineurs à Scranton, en Pennsylvanie.

C'est au travail que les femmes vécurent les changements les plus importants. Durant la guerre, elles se mirent à conduire des bus, à livrer du charbon, à superviser des sections du réseau ferroviaire ; elles devinrent agents de police, soldats ou fermières. Pour ces femmes, ces emplois étaient plus intéressants et plus rentables que tout ce qu'elles avaient fait jusque-là.

(Opposite) Out with the old… the driver of a horse-drawn tram. (Right) …and in with the new – the driver of an electric tram.

(Gegenüberliegende Seite) Weg mit dem Alten … der Fahrer einer Pferdestraßenbahn. (Rechts) … und hin zum Neuen – der Fahrer einer elektrischen Straßenbahn.

(Ci-contre) C'est la fin d'une époque … et des conducteurs de tram tiré par des chevaux. (À droite) Voici du neuf … et un conducteur de tram électrique.

(Left) Releasing the brake – a London bus driver, March 1910. (Opposite) Releasing the slip coach – a guard on a LNWR train detaches the rear car.

(Links) Bremse los – ein Londoner Busfahrer im März 1910. (Gegenüberliegende Seite) Kupplung los – der Schaffner eines Zuges der LNWR hängt den hinteren Waggon ab.

(À gauche) Desserrant le frein – un conducteur de bus londonien, mars 1910. (Ci-contre) Détachant un wagon – un agent des chemins de fer londoniens procède au détachement du wagon arrière.

(Opposite) A conductress on an open-top bus, 1916. (Above) The guard on a Metropolitan train, north London, 28 December 1916. The boots may well have warmed the heart of many a commuter on this cold grey day...

(Gegenüberliegende Seite) Schaffnerin auf dem Oberdeck eines offenen Busses, 1916. (Oben) Die Schaffnerin eines innerstädtischen Zuges in Nord-London, 28. Dezember 1916. Ihre Stiefel mögen an diesem kalten, grauen Tag manchem Pendler das Herz erwärmt haben.

(Ci-contre) Une femme contrôleur sur la plate-forme découverte d'un bus à deux étages, 1916. (Ci-dessus) Une femme agent de métro, au nord de Londres, le 28 décembre 1916. Il est bien possible que sa tenue ait réchauffé le cœur de plus d'un passager en ce jour froid et gris ...

Work for all. Men looking for work queue at the new Labour Exchange, Camberwell Green, London, February 1910. Labour exchanges were established to help casual workers find employment.

Arbeit für alle. Arbeitssuchende stehen Schlange auf dem neuen Arbeitsamt, Camberwell Green, London, im Februar 1910. Arbeitsämter wurden eingerichtet, um Gelegenheitsarbeitern eine Beschäftigung zu verschaffen.

Du travail pour tous. Des hommes à la recherche d'un emploi font la queue à la nouvelle Bourse de l'Emploi de Camberwell Green (Londres), février 1910. Ces Bourses de l'Emploi furent mises en place pour aider les travailleurs temporaires à trouver du travail.

Free for all. Factory and mill foremen select workers from a crowd of unemployed men. The system was open to much abuse, with preference being given to friends and relations and non-union workers.

Offen für alle. Fabrikvorarbeiter wählen Arbeiter aus einer Menge von Arbeitslosen. Es gab viel Missbrauch in diesem System – Freunde, Verwandte oder nicht gewerkschaftlich organisierte Arbeiter wurden gern bevorzugt.

Ouvert à tous. Des contremaîtres d'usine sélectionnent des ouvriers parmi une foule de chômeurs. Ce système laissait libre cours à tous les abus, la préférence étant donnée aux camarades, connaissances et ouvriers non-syndiqués.

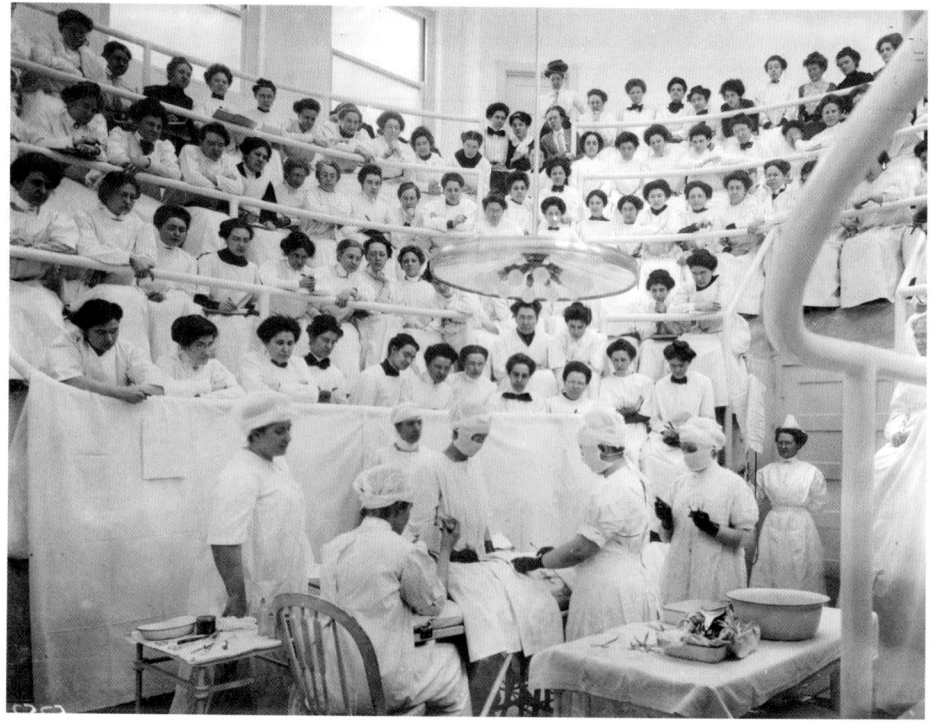

Cutting bodies. Medical students observe the dissection of a corpse at the Women's College Hospital, Philadelphia, March 1911. The provision of higher education for women was steadily advancing in the US, except in the south.

Eingriff in den Körper. Medizinstudentinnen folgen der Sektion einer Leiche im Women's College Hospital, Philadelphia, März 1911. Höhere Bildung stand Frauen in den USA, außer im Süden, in immer größerem Umfang offen.

Dissection d'un corps. Des étudiantes en médecine assistent à une autopsie à l'École de médecine pour femmes de Philadelphie, mars 1911. L'accès des femmes à l'enseignement supérieur se généralisait progressivement aux États-Unis, excepté dans le sud du pays.

Cutting coal. Women coal trimmers in the United States, May 1919.
Their days of industrial work were numbered: the men whom they had
replaced demanded their jobs back when they returned from the war.

Zugriff auf die Kohle. Kohlestauerinnen in den USA, Mai 1919.
Ihre Tage als Industriearbeiterinnen waren gezählt: Die Männer, die
sie ersetzt hatten, verlangten nach ihrer Rückkehr aus dem Krieg ihre
Arbeitsplätze zurück.

Dissection d'une mine. Charbonnières aux États-Unis, mai 1919. Leurs
jours étaient comptés : les hommes qu'elles avaient remplacés pendant
la guerre réclamaient leur emploi une fois de retour de la guerre.

Night mail. Bags of Christmas post are loaded on to a Post Office train at London's Euston Station, bound for Aberdeen, 21 December 1912. Letter-sorting coaches first appeared on British trains in 1838.

Nachtpost. Säcke mit Weihnachtspost werden in Londons Euston Station auf den Postzug nach Aberdeen verladen, 21. Dezember 1912. Sortierwaggons für die Post gab es schon seit 1838 in britischen Zügen.

Courrier de nuit. Chargement de sacs remplis de courrier de Noël à bord d'un train à destination d'Aberdeen, gare de Euston (Londres) le 21 décembre 1912. Ces wagons de distribution postale firent leur apparition sur les trains britanniques en 1838 pour la première fois.

Daily grind. Clerks at work in the offices of a London bus company.
The best qualifications for office work were punctuality, honesty,
copperplate handwriting and a head for figures.

Tagewerk. Angestellte bei der Arbeit im Büro einer Londoner Busgesell-
schaft. Die besten Qualifikationen für Büroarbeit waren Pünktlichkeit,
Ehrlichkeit, eine gestochene Handschrift und ein Sinn für Zahlen.

Train-train quotidien. Employés administratifs d'une compagnie de bus
londonienne. Pour travailler dans un bureau, il fallait avoir les qualités
suivantes : être ponctuel et honnête, avoir une écriture bien ronde et
être doué pour les calculs.

British takeover, female makeover. Women employees at the Short Brothers Works in Southampton patch up the fabric on the inside of a Zeppelin gas bag, February 1919. Women were generally considered better than men at such work.

Britische Übernahme, weibliche Nachbesserung. Weibliche Beschäftigte in den Werken der Short Brothers in Southampton bessern die Hülle eines Zeppelins von innen aus, Februar 1919. Frauen wurden im Allgemeinen als geeigneter für diese Arbeit angesehen als Männer.

Contrôle britannique, reprise féminine. Des employées de Short Brothers Works à Southampton raccommodent le tissu d'un ballon de zeppelin depuis l'intérieur, février 1919. Les femmes étaient généralement considérées comme de meilleures ouvrières que les hommes pour ce genre de travaux.

Popping out for a breath of fresh air. Two of the female workers at the Short Brothers Works, February 1919. The golden age of the airship was about to begin. It lasted little more than a decade.

Auftauchen für etwas Frischluft. Zwei der Arbeiterinnen in den Werken der Short Brothers, Februar 1919. Das goldene Zeitalter des Luftschiffes begann gerade. Es dauerte wenig mehr als ein Jahrzehnt.

Passer la tête dehors pour prendre un bol d'air frais. Deux employées de Short Brothers Works, février 1919. L'âge d'or du dirigeable commençait à peine et dura à peine plus d'une décennie.

Mountains of tea. A team of shovellers blending 48,000lb of tea, 17 September 1916. The tea was later packed into airtight tins and despatched to British troops on the Western Front.

Tee, tonnenweise. Eine Gruppe von Arbeitern mit Schaufeln mischt 48 000 Pfund (ca. 22 000 kg) Tee, 17. September 1916. Der Tee wurde später in luftdichte Dosen verpackt und an die britischen Truppen an der Westfront verschickt.

Montagnes de thé. Une équipe d'hommes équipés de pelles mélangent 22 000 kg de thé, 17 septembre 1916. Le thé était ensuite emballé sous vide dans des boîtes en fer et envoyé aux troupes britanniques sur le front Ouest.

Cups of tea. Women maintenance workers at the Gas Light and Coke Company Works, Bromley-by-Bow, London, take a tea break on top of one of the gas holders, 11 June 1918.

Tee, tassenweise. Wartungsarbeiterinnen der Gas Light and Coke Company in Bromley-by-Bow, London, machen am 11. Juni 1918 eine Teepause auf einem der Gasbehälter.

Tasses de thé. Des employées affectées à l'entretien pour Gas Light and Coke Company Works font une pause en buvant une tasse de thé sur le toit d'un des gazomètres de la compagnie à Bromley-by-Bow (Londres), le 11 juin 1918.

9. Leisure
Freizeit
Les loisirs

Hold on to your hats! Visitors to the fairground at the Japan-British Exhibition in London enjoy the delights of the 'wibble-wobble' – an early form of dodgem, or bumper car – August 1910.

Hüte festhalten! Besucher des Jahrmarkts der japanisch-britischen Ausstellung genießen die Vergnügungen des „Wibble-Wobble" – einer Frühform des Autoscooters – im August 1910.

Tenez bien vos chapeaux ! Des visiteurs à la fête foraine de l'Exposition britannico-japonaise à Londres savourent les frissons d'un tour en « chaises branlantes », une version ancienne des autos tamponneuses, août 1910.

9. Leisure
Freizeit
Les loisirs

There was little time for leisure with a six-day working week, but with a few shillings in your purse or pocket there was joy to be found even on a Sunday. Clerks and mill-hands, shop-girls and apprentices flocked to the country or the seaside, breathed clean air, drank a little beer, munched their pies and sandwiches and enjoyed fleeting romance on the last train or bus home. For Sunday cyclists, the roads were gloriously empty. For anglers, rivers, lakes and streams were well-stocked and unpolluted. On moors and mountains there was space to set up a tent and no need to ask permission.

If the purse or pocket held bank notes then 'leisure' meant more than just the occasional day off. The wealthy spent entire seasons in country retreats, in villas by the sea, in fine houses at the heart of great cities. There were parties, balls, shoots, concerts, regattas, hunts, amateur theatricals, tennis parties and a host of activities to delight and exhaust.

War permitting, the adventurous could pursue the pleasures of the entire planet – climbing in the Alps, excursions to the ruins of Rome and Greece, cruises to the Orient, safaris in Africa… the list was endless.

Eine Sechs-Tage-Woche ließ wenig Raum für Freizeit, aber mit ein bisschen Kleingeld in der Börse oder Hosentasche konnte man auch an einem Sonntag Spaß haben. Büroangestellte und Fabrikarbeiter, Ladenmädchen und Lehrjungen schwärmten aufs Land oder an die Küste aus, atmeten saubere Luft ein, tranken etwas Bier, futterten fröhlich ihre Pasteten oder Sandwiches auf und genossen eine flüchtige Romanze im letzten Zug oder Bus nach Hause. Wer sonntags Rad fahren wollte, fand phantastisch leere Straßen vor. Für Angler waren die Flüsse, Seen und Bäche reich gefüllt und schadstofffrei. In den Mooren und auf Bergen war Platz genug, ein Zelt aufzustellen, ohne dass man um Erlaubnis fragen musste.

Wenn Börse oder Tasche auch Banknoten enthielten, bedeutete „Freizeit" mehr als ein gelegentlicher freier Tag. Die Reichen verbrachten die Saison auf Landsitzen, in Villen am Meer, in schönen Häusern im Herzen der Großstädte. Es gab Partys, Bälle, Schießwettbewerbe, Konzerte, Regatten, Jagden, Amateurtheater-Aufführungen, Tennisveranstaltungen und alle möglichen anderen Betätigungen, die bis zur Erschöpfung Spaß machten.

Sofern der Krieg es zuließ, konnten Abenteuerlustige weltweit die Vergnügungsangebote genießen – Bergsteigen in den Alpen, Exkursionen zu den antiken Stätten in Rom und Griechenland, Kreuzfahrten in den Orient, Safaris in Afrika … die Liste nahm kein Ende.

La semaine de six jours ne laissait guère de temps libre pour les loisirs. Mais il suffisait d'avoir quelques shillings dans son porte-monnaie pour s'amuser, même un dimanche. Employés et ouvriers des filatures, vendeuses et apprentis se rendaient en masse à la campagne ou au bord de la mer pour respirer le bon air, boire un peu de bière, croquer une quiche ou un sandwich et vivre une brève romance sur le trajet du retour à la maison, par le dernier train ou bus. Les cyclistes du dimanche circulaient sur des routes fabuleusement désertes. Les pêcheurs pêchaient dans des rivières, des lacs et des ruisseaux non pollués où le poisson abondait. Dans les landes et les collines, il y avait assez de place pour installer sa tente et il n'était pas nécessaire d'en demander l'autorisation.

Si votre portefeuille était bien garni de billets de banque, alors «divertissement» signifiait plus qu'un jour de congé accordé par-ci par-là. Les riches passaient des saisons entières dans leurs maisons de campagne, leurs villas au bord de la mer ou dans leurs belles demeures au centre des grandes villes. Ils organisaient des fêtes, des bals, des parties de chasse, des concerts, des régates, des chasses à courre, des pièces de théâtre amateur, des parties de tennis et une multitude d'activités pour s'amuser et s'épuiser.

Et si la guerre le permettait malgré tout, les aventuriers pouvaient s'adonner aux plaisirs de la planète entière, escalader les Alpes, faire des excursions parmi les ruines romaines et grecques, entreprendre des croisières en Orient ou des safaris en Afrique… la liste était inépuisable.

Messing about on
the river. A large
Kodak 'bellows'
camera is about to
capture the delights
of punting, 1910.

Spaß auf dem Fluss.
Eine große Kodak-
Balgenkamera
wird in Anschlag
gebracht, um die
Freuden einer
Paddelpartie
einzufangen, 1910.

Passer son temps sur
la rivière. Un grand
Kodak à soufflets est
sur le point de saisir
les délices d'une
promenade en
bateau, 1910.

Fringe of the ocean. Two bathers on the beach at Ostend, Belgium, 1911. The one-piece bathing costume had by then been accepted in all but the most conservative of resorts.

Meeressaum. Zwei Badende am Strand von Ostende, Belgien, 1911. Der einteilige Badeanzug galt damals nur noch in stockkonservativen Badeorten als inakzeptabel.

Au bord de l'océan. Deux baigneurs sur la plage d'Ostende (Belgique), 1911. Le port du maillot une pièce était désormais accepté partout, sauf dans les stations balnéaires les plus conservatrices.

Heart of London, heat of summer. Bold young women cool off in the Serpentine, Hyde Park, 1911. Tucking one's skirt into one's bloomers was as far as a lady could possibly go.

Im Herzen von London, in der Hitze des Sommers. Kühne junge Frauen kühlen sich in der Serpentine ab, dem künstlich angelegten See im Hyde Park, 1911. Den Rock aufzukrempeln und in den Bund der Pumphosen zu stecken war ungefähr das Äußerste, was sich eine Lady erlauben durfte.

Au cœur de Londres, chaleur d'été. Des jeunes femmes bien téméraires se rafraîchissent dans la Serpentine à Hyde Park, 1911. Une demoiselle ne pouvait guère faire mieux que de remonter sa jupe dans ses culottes bouffantes.

Over-exposed. A naked swimmer is caught by the camera as he wades into the moonlit sea at Westcliff-on-Sea, Essex, during a heat wave in the summer of 1911. Such hedonistic depravity was frowned upon.

Allzu frei. Ein nackter Schwimmer wird von der Kamera ertappt, als er während einer Hitzewelle im Sommer 1911 in das vom Mond erleuchtete Meer bei Westcliff-on-Sea in Essex watet. Eine solche hedonistische Verderbtheit erregte Stirnrunzeln.

Surexposé. Un nageur tout nu est saisi par un appareil photo alors qu'il patauge dans la mer éclairée par la lune à Westcliff-on-Sea (Essex) durant une vague de chaleur au cours de l'été 1911. Ce genre de débauche hédoniste était mal vu.

Overjoyed. Delighted amateur photographers focus on royal prey during a visit by Edward, Prince of Wales, to Lytham St Anne's, Lancashire, 8 September 1919. The Prince was on a tour of northern England.

Überglücklich. Entzückte Fotoamateure stellen bei einem Besuch von Edward, dem Prince of Wales, in Lytham St. Anne's, Lancashire, die Kameras auf königliche Beute ein, 8. September 1919. Der Prinz war auf einer Rundreise durch Nordengland.

Surexcitation. Ravies, des photographes amateurs ajustent leurs appareils sur leur proie royale, Édouard, Prince de Galles, en visite à Lytham St Anne's (Lancashire), le 8 septembre 1919. Le prince effectuait un tour du nord de l'Angleterre.

Window shopping in the West End of London, 1912. There were no shortages of supply – gowns, shoes, food, furnishings, toys, wines, hats, jewellery… You could buy anything you liked, so long as you had money.

Schaufensterbummel im Londoner West End, 1912. Es gab keine Versorgungsengpässe – Kleider, Schuhe, Lebensmittel, Möbel, Spielzeug, Weine, Hüte, Schmuck … Man konnte kaufen, was man wollte, sofern man das Geld dafür hatte.

Lèche-vitrine dans le West End de Londres, 1912. Il n'y avait pas de rupture de stock – robes, chaussures, nourriture, meubles, jouets, vins, chapeaux, bijoux … Vous pouviez acheter tout ce que vous souhaitiez, si vous en aviez les moyens.

The interior of the extremely popular Mudie's Lending Library, London. The library was founded in 1840 by Charles Edward Mudie, stationer, publisher and bookseller.

Die überaus beliebte Leihbibliothek Mudie's Lending Library in London von innen. Die Bücherei wurde 1840 von dem Papierwarenhändler, Buchhändler und Verleger Charles Edward Mudie gegründet.

Intérieur de la très populaire bibliothèque de prêt Mudie, Londres. Elle fut fondée en 1840 par Charles Edward Mudie, papetier, éditeur et libraire.

Ready, steady… cook! A group of pastrycooks take part in the piemakers' dash, 1910. The venue looks a little on the grand scale for any village fête: this is possibly the 'Office Sports Day'.

Auf die Plätze, fertig … backen! Ein Schwarm Konditorinnen nimmt am Tortenlauf teil, 1910. Die Veranstaltung sieht für ein gewöhnliches Dorffest etwas zu groß aus: Hier handelt es sich vielleicht um den „Betriebssporttag".

Prêt, partez… cuisinez ! Groupe de pâtissières participant à la course des quiches, 1910. L'endroit semble un peu grand pour une simple fête de village. Il s'agit peut-être d'une « journée de joutes sportives » réservée aux employés.

Girls from the Greycoat Hospital School show their skills and suppleness in a display of Swedish drill, April 1914. It was all part of the campaign to ensure *(wo)mens sana in corpore sano*.

Schülerinnen der Greycoat Hospital School zeigen Können und Gelenkigkeit bei gymnastischen Übungen, April 1914. Das gehörte alles zu einem Förderprogramm, nach dem *(wo)mens sana in corpore sano* gelten sollte.

Des élèves de l'école d'infirmières de l'Hôpital de Greycoat s'adonnent à un exercice de gymnastique suédois pour montrer leurs talents et souplesse, avril 1914. Cela faisait partie d'une campagne prônant *(wo)mens sana in corpore sano*.

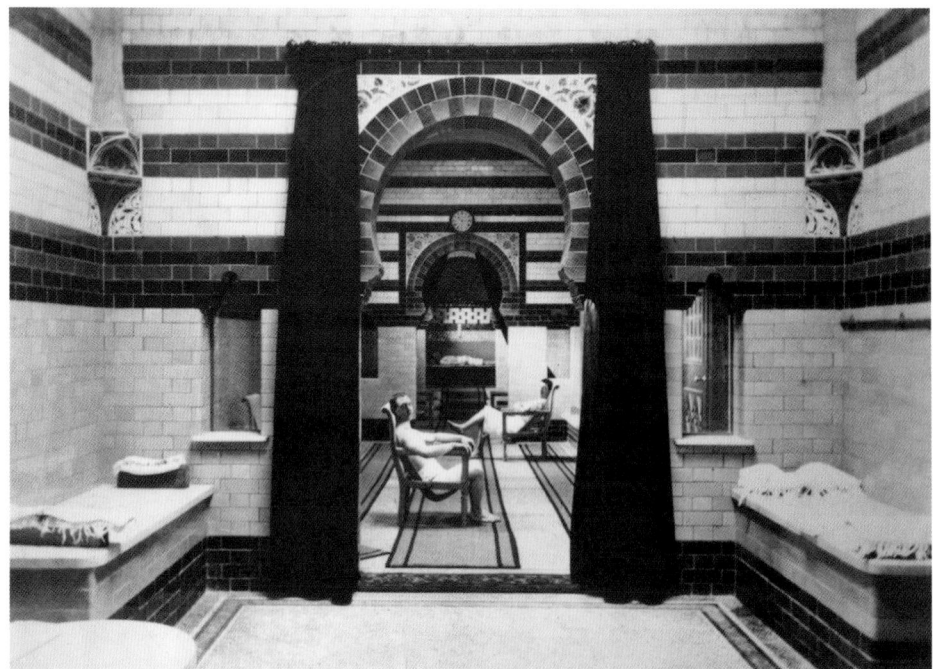

The marbled halls of the new public baths, Harrogate, Yorkshire, 1910. This grand building was not necessarily for those who could not afford a bathroom at home. It served as an informal club for the Spa's middle classes.

Die gefliesten Hallen der neuen öffentlichen Bäder in Harrogate, Yorkshire, 1910. Dieses großzügige Gebäude war nicht etwa für diejenigen da, die sich zu Hause kein Badezimmer leisten konnten. Es diente als formloser Club für die bürgerliche Mittelschicht des Badeortes.

Les salles marbrées des nouveaux bains publics de Harrogate (Yorkshire), 1910.
Ce grand complexe n'était pas forcément destiné à ceux qui, faute de moyens, n'avaient pas de salle de bains chez eux. Il servait de club informel aux classes moyennes de la station thermale.

Work-out on the waves. The gymnasium on board the Cunard liner RMS *Franconia*, 21 February 1911. The equipment looks comparatively modern, the clothing absurdly unsuitable.

Fitness auf hoher See. Der Sportraum an Bord der RMS *Franconia*, einem Cunard-Liniendampfer, 21. Februar 1911. Die Ausstattung wirkt vergleichsweise modern, die Bekleidung grotesk unangemessen.

Séance d'entraînement sur l'océan. La salle de gymnastique du paquebot RMS *Franconia* dispose d'un équipement relativement moderne, mais la tenue des sportifs semble complètement inadaptée, 21 février 1911.

Skaters take to
the ice, Oxford,
30 January 1912.
Europe was still in
the middle of what
almost amounted
to a mini Ice Age.

Schlittschuhläufer
wagen sich aufs
Eis, Oxford,
30. Januar 1912.
Europa steckte
mitten in einer Art
Mini-Eiszeit.

Des patineurs
s'adonnent aux
plaisirs du patinage,
Oxford, 30 janvier
1912. L'Europe
était en plein milieu
d'un hiver compa-
rable à un mini-âge
de glace !

Tobogganing down the 'New Run' at Buxton in Derbyshire's Peak District, November 1912. Most children in Europe experienced enough snow and ice to master the arts of sledging and skating.

Rodeln auf der neuen Bahn in Buxton im Peak-Distrikt von Derbyshire, November 1912. Die meisten Kinder in Europa erlebten genug Schnee und Eis, um Übung in den Künsten des Schlittenfahrens und Schlittschuhlaufens zu bekommen.

Partie de luge sur la « nouvelle piste » de Buxton dans le Peak District du Derbyshire, novembre 1912. En Europe, il tomba assez de neige et il gela suffisamment pour que la majorité des enfants deviennent des as du patinage et de la luge.

A Guards officer and his partner waltz around a frozen pond in a London park, 7 February 1919. The scene is probably St James's Park, just across the road from Wellington Barracks.

Ein Gardeoffizier und seine Partnerin beim Eiswalzer auf einem See in einem Londoner Park, 7. Februar 1919. Das Bild zeigt wahrscheinlich den St. James's Park, der nur einen Steinwurf von den Wellington-Kasernen entfernt ist.

Un officier de la Garde et sa partenaire valsent sur un étang gelé dans un parc londonien, le 7 février 1919. Cette scène se déroule probablement à St James's Park, juste en face des baraquements de Wellington.

Firing from the shoulder, the hip and somewhere in between, lady gunners blast away at pheasants in the autumn of 1910. Where could a man find shelter from this monstrous battalion of women?

Schießen aus der Hüfte, aus der Schulter und irgendwo dazwischen: Schützinnen feuern im Herbst 1910 auf Fasane. Wohin sollten sich Männer vor diesem fürchterlichen Frauenbataillon verkriechen?

Prêtes à tirer, le fusil sur l'épaule, la hanche ou au milieu, ces dames chassent le faisan, automne 1910. Où donc un homme pourrait-il se cacher pour échapper à un bataillon de femmes aussi enragé ?

A time out of war… Two attendants find shelter and boredom at a clay pigeon shoot, 1910. Their smart white coats make it easier for the 'shots' to spot them should they wish for livelier game.

Pause im Gefecht … Zwei Helfer finden Schutz und Langeweile beim Tontaubenschießen. Die feschen weißen Jacketts sind eine Hilfestellung für Paradeschützen, die vielleicht auf lebhafteres Wild aus sind.

Une époque sans guerre … Deux rabatteurs trouvent refuge et ennui dans une cabane d'un terrain de tir au pigeon, 1910. Leurs élégantes vestes blanches rendent la tâche plus facile pour les tireurs en mal de gibier plus vivant …

10. Entertainment and the arts
Unterhaltung und die Künste
Les divertissements et les arts

Four members of the Beauty Chorus gather round the horn microphone at Columbia Records, January 1916. The early wax cylinder had long been replaced by the shellac disc.

Vier Mitglieder des Beauty Chorus scharen sich bei der Plattenfirma Columbia Records um das Trichtermikrofon, Januar 1916. Der Wachszylinder früherer Zeit war längst durch die Schellackplatte ersetzt worden.

Quatre membres du Beauty Chorus rassemblés autour d'un microphone en forme de corne de la compagnie Columbia Records, janvier 1916. Le cylindre en cire des débuts avait depuis longtemps été remplacé par le disque en gomme laque.

10. Entertainment and the arts
Unterhaltung und die Künste
Les divertissements et les arts

The demarcation line between entertainment and art – seldom clearly defined – became distinctly fuzzy in the 1910s. The new gramophone brought music of all varieties into millions of homes, with the recorded voices of George Robey and Enrico Caruso, Dame Clara Butt and Mistinguett echoing through tenements, semis and country houses. There were grand operas, light operas, operettas and musical comedies.

The cinema produced its first masterpieces and threatened the theatre's monopoly on drama. D W Griffith established his reputation with *The Birth of a Nation* and *Intolerance* in 1915 and 1916 respectively. Erich Pommer brought post-war regard for the German film industry with *The Cabinet of Dr Caligari* in 1919.

There were great novelists and great playwrights in profusion: Mann and Hauptmann, Shaw and Synge, H G Wells and D H Lawrence, Barbusse and Proust, Wharton and Dreiser, Kafka and Joyce, and a hundred others. Poets poured the passion of anti-war hatred into the verse they scribbled on scraps of paper while in the trenches. Artists opened the eyes of the world with new concepts in sculpture and painting.

And in 1914 Edgar Rice Burroughs created Tarzan of the Apes.

Die Grenze zwischen Kunst und Unterhaltung – selten genug klar definiert – wurde nach 1910 ausgesprochen unscharf. Das neue Grammophon brachte Musik jeglicher Art in die Häuser von Millionen, und die aufgezeichneten Stimmen von George Robey und Enrico Caruso, Dame Clara Butt und Mistinguett klangen in den Wohnungen, Reihenhäusern und Landhäusern wider. Es gab große Opern, leichte Opern, Operetten und Musikkomödien.

Das Kino brachte seine ersten Meisterwerke hervor und bedrohte das Schauspiel-monopol der Bühne. D. W. Griffith begründete seinen Ruf mit *The Birth of a Nation* (1915) und *Intolerance* (1916). Erich Pommer erntete Nachkriegslorbeeren für die deutsche Filmindustrie mit der Produktion von *Das Kabinett des Dr. Caligari* im Jahre 1919.

Große Erzähler und große Dramatiker gab es in Hülle und Fülle: Mann und Hauptmann, Shaw und Synge, H. G. Wells und D. H. Lawrence, Barbusse und Proust, Wharton und Dreiser, Kafka und Joyce und noch 100 weitere. Dichter verwandelten den leidenschaftlichen Hass gegen den Krieg in Verse, die sie in den Schützengräben auf Papierfetzen kritzelten. Bildende Künstler öffneten der Welt mit neuen Auffassungen von Skulptur und Malerei die Augen.

Und natürlich erschuf Edgar Rice Burroughs im Jahr 1914 Tarzan, den Herrn des Dschungels.

La ligne de démarcation entre art et variétés qui n'avait jamais été clairement définie devint encore plus floue dans les années 1910. Le nouveau gramophone permit à des millions de foyers de découvrir les divers styles de musique. Les voix enregistrées de George Robey et Enrico Caruso, Dame Clara Butt et Mistinguett se mirent à résonner dans les immeubles, les maisons jumelées et les maisons de campagne. On y jouait des grands opéras, des opérettes et des comédies musicales.

Le cinéma produisit ses premiers chefs-d'œuvre, mettant en péril le monopole dramatique du théâtre. D. W. Griffith confirma sa réputation avec *Naissance d'une nation* en 1915 et *Intolérance* en 1916. Avec *Le cabinet du Dr Caligari* réalisé en 1919, Erich Pommer donna au cinéma allemand d'après-guerre ses premières lettres de noblesse.

Il y eut une profusion de grands romanciers et de grands dramaturges : Mann et Hauptmann, Shaw et Synge, H. G. Wells et D. H. Lawrence, Barbusse et Proust, Wharton et Dreiser, Kafka et Joyce, et une centaine d'autres. Les poètes déversèrent leur haine de la guerre dans des poèmes dont les vers avaient été gribouillés sur des morceaux de papier au fond des tranchées. Les artistes ouvrirent les yeux du monde en appliquant de nouveaux concepts à la sculpture et à la peinture.

Enfin, en 1914, Edgar Rice Burroughs créa l'histoire de Tarzan.

The Russian ballerina Anna Pavlova with Laurent Mouikov in *Bacchanale*, 1913.
The ballet was danced to music from *Samson et Dalila* by Saint-Saëns. Pavlova was
then at the height of her fame as a dancer.

Die russische Ballerina Anna Pawlowa mit ihrem Partner Laurent Mouikow in
Bacchanale, 1913. Das Ballett wurde zu Musik aus *Samson et Dalila* von Saint-Saëns
getanzt. Die Pawlowa stand damals auf der Höhe ihres tänzerischen Ruhmes.

La ballerine russe Anna Pavlova avec Laurent Mouikov dans *Bacchanales*, 1913.
Le ballet était accompagné d'une musique adaptée de *Samson et Dalila* de Saint-Saëns.
Pavlova était alors au sommet de sa gloire.

Vera Fokina and
Michail Fokine in
the Ballets Russes
production of
Rimsky-Korsakov's
Sheherazade, 1910.

Vera Fokina und
Michail Fokine in
der Aufführung von
Rimski-Korsakows
Scheherazade der
Ballets Russes 1910.

Vera Fokine et
Michel Fokine dans
une production de
Schéhérazade de
Rimsky-Korsakov des
Ballets russes, 1910.

(Opposite) Pavlova poses amid floral tributes at the Ritz Hotel, London, May 1912. (Right) Vaslav Nijinsky in *Le Spectre de la rose*, 1915.

(Gegenüberliegende Seite) Die Pawlowa posiert im Ritz inmitten der Blumen, die sie von Bewunderern erhalten hat, Mai 1912. (Rechts) Waslaw Nijinskij in *Le Spectre de la rose*, 1915.

(Ci-contre) Pavlova photographiée au milieu de fleurs reçues d'admirateurs au Ritz Hotel à Londres, mai 1912. (À droite) Vaslav Nijinsky dans *Le Spectre de la rose*, 1915.

Pierrots and pierrettes pose for a publicity shot on the open top of a bus outside the Drury Lane Theatre in London's West End, April 1915.

Pierrots und Pierretten posieren für eine Werbeaufnahme auf dem offenen Obergeschoss eines Busses vor dem Drury Lane Theatre im Londoner West End, April 1915.

Des Pierrots et des Pierrettes posent pour une publicité sur la plate-forme d'un bus devant le Drury Lane Theatre dans le West End à Londres, avril 1915.

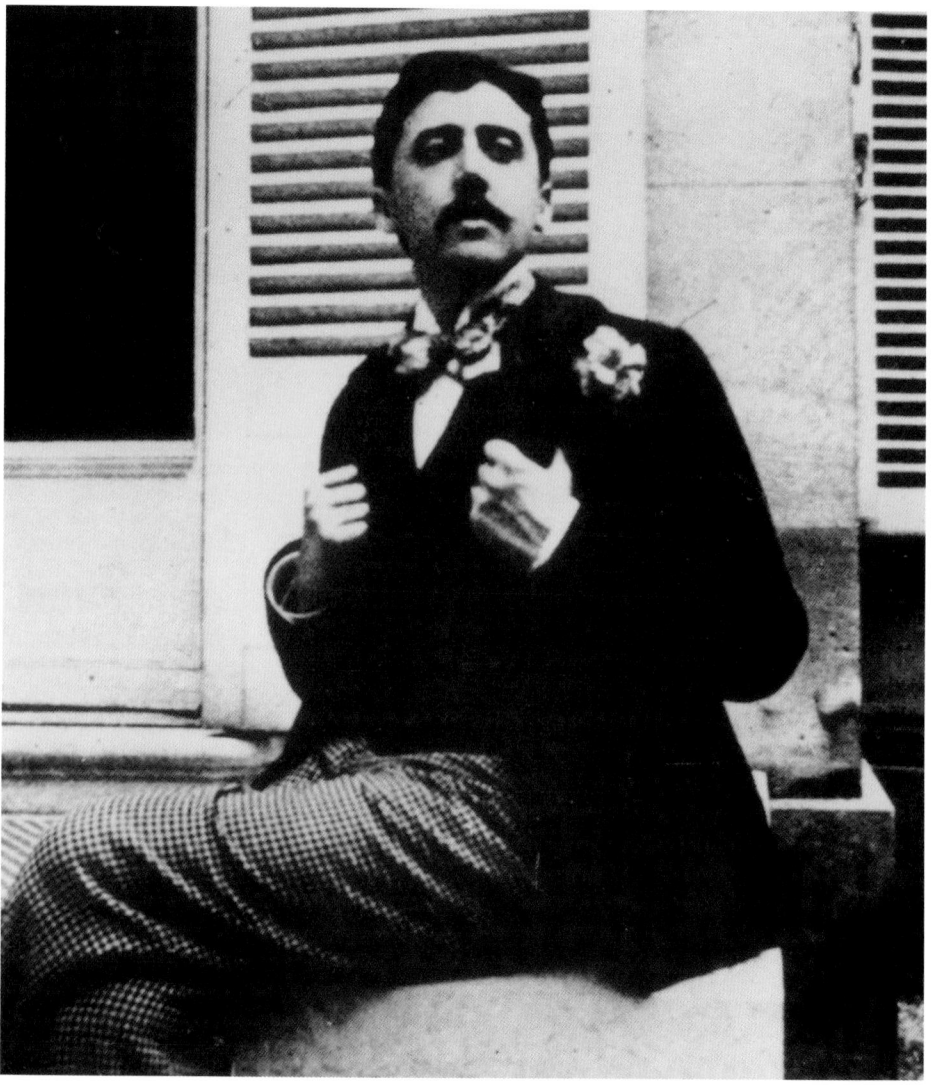

(Opposite) Marcel Proust leaves the sound-proof flat in which he wrote to pose outside a window, 1910. (Above) The French novelist Colette with feline friends, 1910.

(Gegenüberliegende Seite) Marcel Proust hat die schallisolierte Wohnung, in der er schrieb, verlassen, um sich vor einem Fenster dem Fotografen zu stellen. (Oben) Die französische Romanschriftstellerin Colette mit ihren Freunden, den Katzen, 1910.

(Ci-contre) Marcel Proust a quitté son appartement insonorisé dans lequel il écrit pour poser dehors devant une fenêtre, 1910. (Ci-dessus) La romancière française Colette avec ses amis les chats, 1910.

Emilio Filippo Tommaso Marinetti, writer and founder of the Futurist movement, 1915. Marinetti glorified speed, 'dynamism' and, above all, war. In 1919 he joined the Italian Fascists.

Emilio Filippo Tommaso Marinetti, Schriftsteller und Begründer der futuristischen Bewegung, 1915. Marinetti glorifizierte Geschwindigkeit, „Dynamismus" und, vor allem, den Krieg. Im Jahr 1919 schloss er sich den italienischen Faschisten an.

Emilio Filippo Tommaso Marinetti, écrivain et fondateur du mouvement futuriste, 1915. Marinetti glorifiait la vitesse, le « dynamisme » et, avant tout, la guerre. En 1919, il devint membre du parti fasciste italien.

Luigi Russolo and his assistant Piatti prepare the noise machine that performed Russolo's 'Futurist' symphonies, 1913. One of them was staged at the London Coliseum in June 1914.

Luigi Russolo und sein Assistent Piatti stellen die Lärmmaschine auf, mit der Russolos „futuristische" Sinfonien vorgetragen wurden, 1913. Eine davon wurde im London Coliseum im Juni 1914 aufgeführt.

Luigi Russolo et son assistant Piatti mettent au point la machine à bruit qui joua les symphonies 'futuristes' de Russolo, 1913. Une des symphonies fut exécutée au London Coliseum en juin 1914.

Towards the end of his life, Auguste Renoir paints on, 1915. He was almost crippled with arthritis.

Auch gegen Ende seines Lebens malt Auguste Renoir weiter, 1915. Die Arthritis hatte ihn fast vollständig gelähmt.

Vers la fin de sa vie, Auguste Renoir peint encore, 1915. L'arthrite l'avait presque complète-ment paralysé.

Henri Matisse, the founder of the Fauvists, in his Paris studio, 13 May 1913. The days of poverty were now behind him.

Henri Matisse, Begründer des Fauvismus, in seinem Pariser Studio, 13. Mai 1913. Die Zeit der Armut lag jetzt hinter ihm.

Henri Matisse, le chef de file des fauves, dans son atelier parisien, le 13 mai 1913. Les jours de pauvreté étaient maintenant derrière lui.

James Montgomery Flagg stands proudly beside his famous recruiting poster, 1918. It was based on an earlier British poster of Kitchener.

James Montgomery Flagg steht stolz neben seinem berühmten Rekrutierungsplakat, 1918. Die Vorlage bildete ein früheres britisches Plakat von Kitchener.

James Montgomery Flagg se tient fièrement à côté de sa célèbre affiche en faveur de la mobilisation, 1918. Elle fut inspirée par une affiche plus ancienne du Britannique Kitchener.

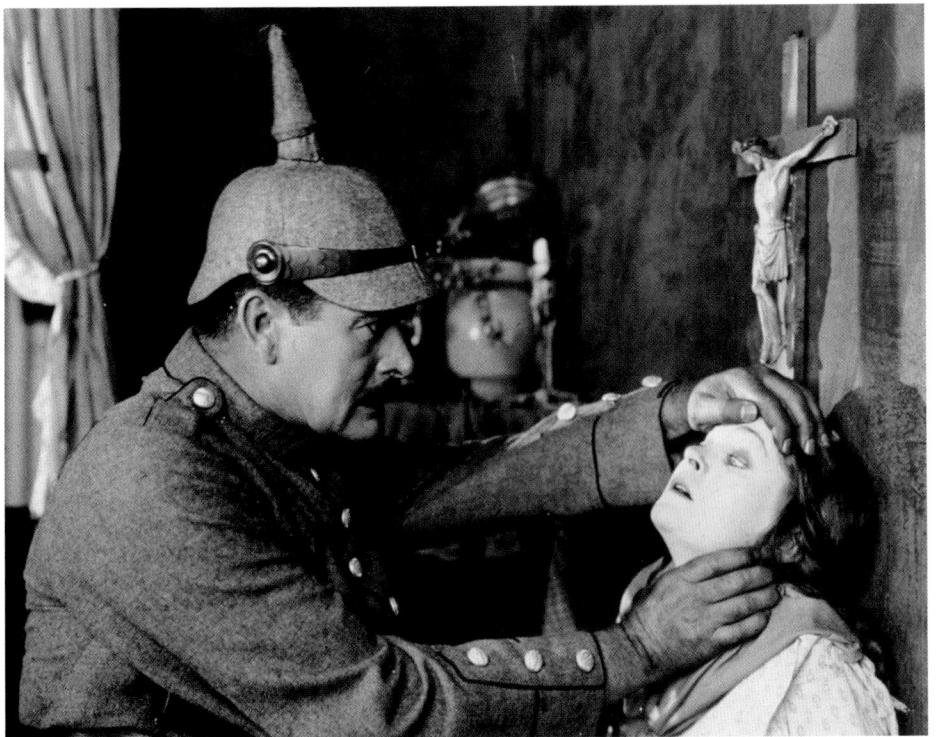

A still from a typical anti-German MGM film of 1918. Most governments quickly realised the powerful role that cinema could play in the war of propaganda, and encouraged studios to make such films.

Standfoto aus einem typischen antideutschen Film der MGM von 1918. Die meisten Regierungen erkannten schnell die wichtige Rolle, die das Kino im Propagandakrieg spielen konnte und ermunterten die Filmgesellschaften, solche Filme zu drehen.

Scène d'un film anti-allemand typique produit par la MGM en 1918. La plupart des gouvernements prirent rapidement conscience du rôle puissant que pouvait jouer le cinéma dans la guerre de propagande et encouragèrent les studios à réaliser de tels films.

For King and Country... The American-born British sculptor Jacob Epstein in uniform, 1917.

Für König und Vaterland ... Der in Amerika geborene britische Bildhauer Jacob Epstein in Uniform, 1917.

Pour le roi et le pays ... Le sculpteur britannique d'origine américaine Jacob Epstein pose en uniforme, 1917.

For Uncle Sam
and Broadway...
The Russian-born
US composer Irving
Berlin in costume
for *Over There*,
1918.

Für Uncle Sam und
den Broadway ...
Der in Russland
geborene amerika-
nische Komponist
Irving Berlin,
kostümiert für
Over There, 1918.

Pour l'Oncle Sam
et Broadway ... Le
compositeur améri-
cain d'origine russe
Irving Berlin pose
en costume pour
Over There, 1918.

A typical scene from the early screen melodrama *The Telegrapher's Daughter*, 1914. The heroine appears doomed, but note the conveniently placed points: they should guarantee her survival.

Eine typische Szene aus dem frühen Leinwandmelodram *The Telegrapher's Daughter,* 1914. Die Heldin scheint dem Untergang geweiht, aber Obacht! Zufällig sind die Weichen richtig gestellt und ihr Überleben ist gesichert.

Scène classique d'un des premiers mélodrames portés au cinéma, *The Telegrapher's Daughter,* 1914. L'héroïne semble condamnée, mais la mise en scène est astucieuse : l'intersection des rails devrait lui permettre d'échapper à une mort tragique.

The famous Keystone Kops, created and directed by Mack Sennett, 1913. On the left, with the telephone, is Ford Sterling. On the far right is a young Roscoe 'Fatty' Arbuckle.

Die berühmten Keystone Kops, Idee und Regie Mack Sennett, 1913. Links, am Telefon, Ford Sterling. Ganz rechts außen ein jugendlicher Roscoe „Fatty" Arbuckle.

Les célèbres Keystone Kops, créés et mis en scène par Mack Sennett, 1913. À gauche, au téléphone, on trouve Ford Sterling et, tout à droite, le jeune Roscoe « Fatty » Arbuckle.

(Above) Giants of the early cinema on the day they formed the United Artists corporation, 17 April 1919. (From left to right) Douglas Fairbanks Snr, David Wark Griffith, Mary Pickford and Charlie Chaplin. (Opposite) Chaplin operates a movie camera, 1915.

(Oben) Giganten des frühen Kinos am 17. April 1919, dem Tag, an dem sie die Filmgesellschaft United Artists gründeten. Douglas Fairbanks Senior, David Wark Griffith, Mary Pickford und Charlie Chaplin (von links nach rechts). (Gegenüberliegende Seite) Chaplin bedient die Filmkamera, 1915.

(Ci-dessus) Les géants des débuts du cinéma photographiés le jour où ils créèrent United Artists Corporation, le 17 avril 1919. (De gauche à droite) Douglas Fairbanks Senior, David Wark Griffith, Mary Pickford et Charlie Chaplin. (Ci-contre) Chaplin derrière la caméra, 1915.

11. Fashion
Mode
La mode

A string of pearls, a Cupid's bow and perfect poise. Socialite Lady Diana Manners, daughter of the 8th Duke of Rutland, shows the general public what it takes to achieve grace and beauty, 1916.

Eine Perlenkette, eine fein gezeichnete Oberlippe und graziöse Körperhaltung. Lady Diana Manners, Mitglied der feinen Gesellschaft und Tochter des Achten Herzogs von Rutland, führt der breiten Öffentlichkeit vor, was Anmut und Schönheit ist, 1916.

Un collier de perles, la bouche en cœur et une pose parfaite. La très mondaine Lady Diana Manners, fille du 8e duc de Rutland, révèle au grand public à quoi riment grâce et beauté, 1916.

11. Fashion
Mode
La mode

No man out of uniform could hope to be called 'fashionable'. No matter how well cut the suit, how stiff the collar, how tightly-knotted the tie, what mattered was the colour of the cloth. The best to be had were the khaki of the British subaltern, the field grey of the German *Hauptmann*, or the powder blue of the French lieutenant. The most a man in civvies could hope for was a curt nod, or a frigid smile, while his brother-in-arms could successfully offer his arm to the most elegantly clad young ladies.

Women, too, took to uniforms. Nurses attained a glamour that film stars sought to emulate. It was chic to wear tunics, epaulettes, brass buttons, caps, *képis* and fur helmets; to adopt a shorter hairstyle; even to don mannish attire.

For a night of splendour, however, the fighting man home on leave wanted a taste and a sight of luxury. It was the time to dress in one's finery, to highlight perfect cheekbones, eyebrows, lips. At balls and dances and in theatres came those delicious moments when the orchestra struck up the hit melody from the latest musical comedy, life assumed its pre-war glamour, and young love stepped out…

Kein Mann ohne Uniform konnte sich Hoffnungen machen, als „modisch" zu gelten. Es spielte keine Rolle wie gut der Anzug geschnitten war, wie steif der Kragen, wie eng gebunden die Krawatte, worauf es wirklich ankam, war die Farbe des Stoffes. Am besten bedient war man mit dem Khaki des britischen Subalternoffiziers, dem Feldgrau des deutschen Hauptmanns oder dem Taubenblau des französischen Leutnants. Ein Mann in Zivil konnte bestenfalls mit einem kurzen Kopfnicken oder einem kühlen Lächeln rechnen, während sein Waffen tragender Bruder den elegantesten jungen Damen voller Zuversicht den Arm bieten durfte.

Auch Frauen trugen gern Uniformen. Krankenschwestern erwarben eine Aura des Glamourösen, der Filmstars mühsam nacheiferten. Es war schick, Uniformröcke, Epauletten, Messingknöpfe, Mützen, Képis und Pelzmützen zu tragen, sich eine Kurzhaarfrisur zuzulegen, ja sogar, sich wie ein Mann zu kleiden.

An einem glanzvollen Abend wollte der Frontkämpfer auf Heimaturlaub jedoch einen Hauch von Luxus sehen und schmecken. Das war die geeignete Stunde, sich prachtvoll zu kleiden, die Vollkommenheit von Wangenknochen, Augenbrauen und Lippen zu betonen. Bei großen Bällen, Tanzveranstaltungen und in Theatern kam es zu jenen zauberhaften Augenblicken, in denen das Orchester die beliebteste Melodie aus der neuesten Musikkomödie anstimmte, das Leben den Glanz der Vorkriegszeit zurückgewann und frisch erblühte Liebe sich zeigen durfte …

Les hommes qui ne portaient pas l'uniforme n'avaient aucun espoir d'être classés parmi les gens « à la mode ». Peu importait la coupe du complet, la rigidité du col, ce qui comptait, c'était la couleur de l'étoffe. Parmi les plus recherchées, il y avait le kaki de l'officier britannique, le gris du commandant allemand et le bleu du lieutenant français. Alors qu'un homme en civil se voyait à peine gratifié d'un léger signe de la tête ou d'un pâle sourire, son frère d'armes ne se voyait jamais refuser le bras d'une jeune femme très élégante.

Les femmes se mirent elles aussi à porter l'uniforme. Les infirmières dégageaient plus de glamour que les stars de cinéma. C'était devenu chic de porter des tuniques, des épaulettes, des boutons en laiton, des capes, des képis et des casques en fourrure, d'opter pour les cheveux courts et même de revêtir une tenue masculine.

Par contre, quand le soldat de retour pour une permission sortait le soir, il voulait goûter au luxe et à la splendeur. Pour les femmes, c'était l'occasion de mettre leurs plus belles tenues, de souligner la perfection des joues, des sourcils et des lèvres. Aux bals, dans les soirées dansantes et aux théâtres, il y avait cet instant magique où l'orchestre entamait l'air de la dernière comédie musicale en vogue, la vie retrouvait alors son charme d'avant-guerre et les amoureux dévoilaient leurs sentiments …

In the first summer of peace, three little maids arrive at Buckingham Palace for a garden party, 16 July 1919. The London Season was well under way, and the maids would have to maintain the freshness of youth against a barrage of late nights.

Im ersten Friedenssommer, 16. Juli 1919, treffen drei junge Damen zu einer Gartengesellschaft im Buckingham Palace ein. Die Londoner Saison war in vollem Gange, und die Debütantinnen mussten die Frische der Jugend gegen allzu viele kurze Nächte verteidigen.

C'est le premier été de l'après-guerre et ces trois demoiselles arrivent au Palais de Buckingham pour une garden-party, le 16 juillet 1919. La saison londonienne était déjà bien entamée et ces jeunes filles auraient à s'en remettre à leur jeunesse pour surmonter les nuits trop courtes.

Stepping out. The 8th Duke of Rutland leaves a private view at the Royal Academy of Art, London, May 1914. The top hat was still *de rigueur* for such events.

Ausgang. Der Achte Herzog von Rutland verlässt die Vorabbesichtigung einer Ausstellung in der Königlichen Akademie der Künste, London, Mai 1914. Bei solchen Gelegenheiten gehörte noch immer der Zylinder zum guten Ton.

Sortie. Le 8ᵉ duc de Rutland quitte une projection privée donnée au Royal Academy of Art, Londres, mai 1914. Le chapeau haut de forme est encore de rigueur lors de tels événements.

Edward, Prince of Wales (at the wheel), sets off with a group of friends for a meet of the beagles of Magdalen College, Oxford, 12 December 1913. The oversized flat caps were extremely fashionable.

Edward, der Prince of Wales (am Steuerrad), fährt mit einer Gruppe von Freunden zu einer Beagle-Jagd, Magdalen College, Oxford, 12. Dezember 1913. Die übergroßen flachen Mützen waren der allerletzte Schrei.

Édouard, prince de Galles (au volant), prêt à partir avec des amis pour une partie de chasse à courre du Magdalen College à Oxford, le 12 décembre 1913. À cette époque, le port des casquettes trop grandes était très en vogue.

Young lady-in-waiting, 1919. Bessie Wallis Spencer (later Edward's wife and Duchess of Windsor) in an elegant summer dress.

Junge Hofdame, 1919. Bessie Wallis Spencer (später Edwards Frau und Herzogin von Windsor) in einem eleganten Sommerkostüm.

Une jeune future lady, 1919. Bessie Wallis Spencer (la future épouse d'Édouard et duchesse de Windsor) vêtue d'une élégante robe d'été.

A young woman skater performs a daring pirouette on a frozen pond in a Berlin park, 15 January 1914.

Eine junge Schlittschuhläuferin vollführt eine gewagte Pirouette auf dem zugefrorenen Teich eines Berliner Parks, 15. Januar 1914.

Une jeune patineuse se permet une pirouette osée sur un étang gelé dans un parc de Berlin, le 15 janvier 1914.

Marguerite and Frank Gill dip and glide their way through an exhibition of the Brazilian maxixe at the Criterion restaurant, London, 7 January 1914. The 'Cri' was very much in vogue at the time.

Marguerite und Frank Gill exerzieren die Gleit- und Beugefiguren des brasilianischen Gesellschaftstanzes Maxixe durch, im Restaurant Criterion in London, 7. Januar 1914. Das „Cri" war damals en vogue.

Marguerite et Frank Gill effectuent un pas de danse lors d'une démonstration de « maxixe » brésilienne, sorte de polka, donnée au Criterion à Londres, le 7 janvier 1914. Le « Cri » était un restaurant très à la mode en ce temps-là.

A summer's day, a picnic hamper, a skiff with plenty of cushions, and a portable gramophone. The wonders of the wind-up, thanks to the Decca Company, create an afternoon of bliss, August 1919.

Ein Sommertag, ein Picknickkorb, ein Kahn mit vielen Kissen und ein tragbares Grammophon. Die Wunder des „Aufziehbaren" verwandeln, dank der Decca-Gesellschaft, einen Nachmittag im August 1919 in pures Glück.

Par une belle journée d'été, il suffit d'une corbeille de pique-nique, d'une barque garnie de coussins et d'un gramophone portatif, grâce aux miracles de Decca, pour passer un après-midi de parfait bonheur, août 1919.

Designers of sporting costumes still placed propriety above comfort. The outfit worn by Miss Kyle at Portrush, County Antrim, Ulster, in May 1911 would appear to be more suitable for ballooning than golf.

Die Designer von Sportkleidung stellten noch immer den Anstand über die Bequemlichkeit. Der Aufzug, in dem Miss Kyle in Portrush, County Antrim, Ulster, im Mai 1911 erscheint, wirkt für eine Ballonfahrt angemessener als für Golf.

Les stylistes de vêtements de sport privilégiaient encore la bienséance au détriment du confort. L'ensemble porté par Mlle Kyle à Portrush (Comté d'Antrim), Ulster, paraît plus adapté pour monter en ballon que jouer au golf, mai 1911.

Madame Reytiens of France leaps across the tennis court, comparatively unimpeded by pleated skirt, long-sleeved blouse and nifty hat, at the Queen's Club, Hurlingham, London, May 1918.

Madame Reytiens aus Frankreich hüpft über den Tennisplatz des Queen's Club, Hurlingham, London, im Mai 1918, augenscheinlich ungehindert durch Plisseerock, langärmlige Bluse und den flotten Hut.

La Française, Madame Reytiens, rebondit sur le court de tennis du Queen's Club (Hurlingham) à Londres, relativement peu gênée par sa jupe plissée, son chemisier à longues manches et son incroyable chapeau, mai 1918.

Even on a cold day by the grey sea on the coast of Britain in 1918, one could be considerably more daring, though it did not do to spend too long out of the water lest one be accused of flaunting oneself.

Selbst an einem kalten Tag an der grauen See der britischen Küste im Jahre 1918 konnte man sich erheblich gewagter geben, auch wenn es nicht ratsam war, allzu lange außerhalb des Wassers zu bleiben, wenn man nicht beschuldigt werden wollte, sich zur Schau zu stellen.

Même par une froide journée au bord d'une mer grise sur la côte britannique en 1918, certains osaient se montrer plus audacieux, bien que cela ne se fît pas de rester trop longtemps hors de l'eau sous peine d'être accusé de faire étalage de sa personne.

Votes for Women! Jobs for Women! Football for Women! What was the world coming to? The Harrodian Ladies Football Team parade at Barnes, 24 November 1917 – long before the present Harrods boss took over Fulham Football Club.

Stimmrecht für Frauen! Arbeitsplätze für Frauen! Fußball für Frauen! Was sollte nur aus der Welt werden? Die Damenfußballmannschaft von Harrods stellt sich am 24. November 1917 in Barnes vor – lange bevor der gegenwärtige Chef von Harrods den Fulham Football Club übernahm.

Droit de vote et travail pour les femmes! Le football pour les femmes aussi! Mais où allait le monde? L'équipe féminine de football de Harrods s'affiche à Barnes, le 24 novembre 1917, bien longtemps avant que l'actuel propriétaire de Harrods prenne la direction du club de football de Fulham.

Even in the 1910s comedians dreamed of being able to make jokes about 'it's a fair cop'. Here was one of their first opportunities. Women police recruits parade in their 'civvies', 30 January 1917…

Zu Beginn des Jahrzehnts träumten Komiker noch davon, Witze über „it's a fair cop" („jetzt hat's mich erwischt/was für ein hübscher Polizist") zu machen. Hier bietet sich eine der ersten Gelegenheiten. Polizeirekrutinnen stellen sich in Zivil auf, am 30. Januar 1917 …

Dans les années 1910 déjà, les comiques britanniques ne manquèrent pas de faire des blagues à propos de l'expression 'it's a fair cop' (qui signifiait à la fois « ce n'est que justice » et « c'est une jolie policière »). En voici une des premières occasions : des nouvelles recrues de la police s'affichent en civil, le 30 janvier 1917 …

…a couple of hours later, the same recruits parade in their uniforms. The unit was attached to a munitions factory, where most of the workforce would have been made up of women.

… und ein paar Stunden später in Uniform. Die Einheit wurde einer Munitionsfabrik zugeteilt, wo die Arbeiterschaft wohl zum größten Teil aus Frauen bestand.

… et, quelques heures plus tard, posent en uniforme. Cette unité était rattachée à une fabrique de munitions dont l'essentiel des employés était constitué de femmes.

The outfits were
not the smartest,
but beauty rather
than fashion was
in the eyes of
the beholders on this
summer's day
in 1910.

Die Kleidung war
nicht eben die
schickste, aber an
diesem Sommertag
wurde über
Geschmack
bestimmt nicht
gestritten, 1910.

Il existait des tenues
plus élégantes, mais,
en cette journée
d'été de 1910,
ce qui comptait le
plus aux yeux de
ce couple était la
beauté et non la
mode.

A young Parisienne
shows off her high-
collared three-
quarter length coat
with bell-cuffs,
November 1916.

Eine junge Pariserin
präsentiert stolz
ihren dreiviertel-
langen Mantel mit
Glockenärmeln und
hohem Kragen,
November 1916.

Une jeune Parisienne
crânant dans son
manteau trois quarts
avec col montant
et manches en
forme de cloche,
novembre 1916.

12. Transport
Verkehr
Les moyens de transport

The robustness of the modern bicycle is tested by those who prefer not to pay to see the Hendon Aviation Meeting, 13 May 1911. It was the largest annual flying display in Britain.

Die Robustheit des modernen Fahrrads wird von denen getestet, die für den Besuch der Luftfahrtausstellung in Hendon am 13. Mai 1911 lieber nichts bezahlen wollen. Es war die größte jährliche Flugschau in Großbritannien.

La solidité des bicyclettes modernes est mise à l'épreuve par ces messieurs qui ont décidé d'assister gratuitement au salon aéronautique de Hendon, le 13 mai 1911. C'était le plus grand salon aéronautique annuel de Grande-Bretagne.

12. Transport
Verkehr
Les moyens de transport

The power and promise of the motor car, the aeroplane and the submarine were revealed. By the end of the decade, flying was sufficiently safe for regular passenger services to be initiated, for mail to travel by air from country to country. The motor car rediscovered forgotten villages and brought an end to the horse-drawn centuries.

The submarine proved its malevolent worth by sending hundreds of other vessels to graveyards at the bottom of the ocean. Claims that an unsinkable ship rode the waves were tragically disproved when the *Titanic* hit an iceberg in 1912; nonetheless, bigger ships carried heavier cargoes and more passengers at greater speeds than ever before.

Trains still brought the masses to work and took them out to play. Railway companies competed in splendour, building stations and accompanying hotels that rivalled medieval cathedrals and had far larger congregations. It was possible to steam through the Alps, to crawl across the Nullarbor Plain, to venture into the Arctic Circle, and to cross every continent on earth, save the Antarctic, by train.

Die Möglichkeiten des Automobils, des Flugzeuges und des Unterseebootes wurden allmählich erkannt. Bis Ende des Jahrzehnts war das Fliegen sicher genug, sodass regelmäßige Passagierflüge eingerichtet und Post auf dem Luftweg von Land zu Land befördert werden konnte. Der Kraftwagen entdeckte vergessene Dörfer wieder und setzte den Jahrhunderten der Pferdestärken ein Ende.

Das U-Boot bewies seinen Nutzen im Bösen, indem es Hunderte anderer Schiffe auf Friedhöfe am Meeresboden schickte. Behauptungen, ein unsinkbares Schiff kreuze die Wellen, wurden tragisch widerlegt, als die *Titanic* 1912 auf einen Eisberg lief; dennoch beförderten immer größere Schiffe immer schneller mehr Frachten und Passagiere.

Noch immer brachten Züge die Massen zur Arbeit und entführten sie in die Freizeit. Die Eisenbahngesellschaften versuchten einander an Prächtigkeit zu übertreffen und bauten Bahnhöfe mit integrierten Hotels, die es mit mittelalterlichen Kathedralen aufnehmen konnten, aber eine größere Gemeinde hatten. Es war möglich, mit Dampfkraft durch die Alpen zu klettern, durch die australische Nullarbor-Wüste zu kriechen, sich zum Polarkreis zu wagen und jeden Kontinent der Erde außer der Antarktis auf Schienen zu durchqueren.

La puissance et l'avenir prometteur de l'automobile, de l'avion et du sous-marin apparurent au grand jour. Au terme de cette décennie, l'avion était devenu un moyen de transport suffisamment sûr pour inaugurer des vols réguliers de passagers et acheminer le courrier par les airs d'un pays à un autre. Quant à l'automobile, elle permit de redécouvrir des villages oubliés et mit fin à des siècles d'attelages tirés par des chevaux.

Le sous-marin révéla sa nature malveillante en envoyant des centaines de navires au fond des océans. Les affirmations selon lesquelles un navire incoulable parcourait les mers furent tragiquement démenties lorsque le *Titanic* heurta un iceberg en 1912. Malgré tout, des navires toujours plus grands transportant des cargaisons toujours plus lourdes et des passagers toujours plus nombreux naviguaient à une vitesse encore jamais atteinte.

Les trains continuaient à transporter les masses sur le lieu de leur travail et de leurs loisirs. Les compagnies de chemin de fer rivalisaient de splendeur, construisant des gares et des hôtels qui rappelaient les cathédrales médiévales dont les congrégations de visiteurs étaient bien plus nombreuses. Il était désormais possible de franchir les Alpes, de traverser la plaine de Nullarbor, de s'aventurer dans le cercle arctique et de traverser tous les continents de la terre en train, à l'exception de l'Antarctique.

A proud and glorious moment – the SS *Titanic* leaves Belfast for her sea trials, April 1912.

Ein stolzer und ruhmreicher Augenblick – die SS *Titanic* läuft zur Überprüfung ihrer Seetauglichkeit im April 1912 aus Belfast aus.

Un moment de fierté et de gloire, le SS *Titanic* quitte Belfast pour des essais en mer, avril 1912.

Ned Parfett sells
newspapers with
details of the tragic
end of the *Titanic*,
16 April 1912.
Six years later he
was killed on the
Western Front.

Ned Parfett
verkauft Zeitungen
mit Einzelheiten
zum tragischen
Ende der *Titanic*,
16. April 1912.
Sechs Jahre später
fiel er an der
Westfront.

Ned Parfett
vend les journaux
relatant la tragique
fin du *Titanic* le
16 avril 1912.
Six ans plus tard,
il mourrait sur le
front Ouest.

End of the line. Men dismantle the bodies of horse-drawn buses, May 1911. Few mourned their passing, and anyway city centres were fast becoming unsuitable for working animals.

Ende der Fahnenstange. Männer zerlegen die Wagen von Pferde-omnibussen, Mai 1911. Wenige bedauerten diesen Abschied, und die Stadtzentren wurden ohnehin für Arbeitstiere immer ungeeigneter.

Fin de parcours. Ces hommes sont occupés à démanteler des « autobus » tirés par des chevaux, mai 1911. La disparition de ce moyen de transport fut peu regrettée, d'autant plus que les centres-villes devinrent très vite inaccessibles aux bêtes de somme.

Start of the day. Rows of new motor buses in the fitting shop of a bus garage, May 1911. Though no faster than their horse-drawn predecessors, they were at least cheaper to run.

Morgenröte. Reihen neuer Motorbusse in der Zubehörwerkstatt einer Busgarage, Mai 1911. Wenn sie auch nicht schneller waren als ihre von Pferden gezogenen Vorgänger, so waren sie wenigstens billiger zu betreiben.

Début de journée. Rangées d'autobus à moteur garés dans le garage du dépôt, mai 1911. Guère plus rapides que leurs ancêtres tirés par des chevaux, ils étaient néanmoins d'un entretien plus économique.

'The only history that is worth a tinker's damn is the history we make today' – Henry Ford. The flywheel assembly line in the new $28,000 Ford motor plant at Highland Park, Detroit, 1914.

„Die einzige Geschichte, die mehr als einen feuchten Kehricht wert ist, ist die Geschichte, die wir heute machen" – Henry Ford. Das Fließband für Schwungräder in der neuen 28 000-Dollar-Motorenfabrik von Ford in Highland Park, Detroit, 1914.

« La seule histoire qui vaille la peine d'être racontée est celle que nous faisons aujourd'hui » – Henry Ford. Chaîne de montage des volants installée dans la nouvelle fabrique de Ford installée à Highland Park (Détroit) pour 28 000 $ en 1914.

The general assembly line at Highland Park. Ford workers were among the highest paid in the United States. At this time the national average wage was $2.40 a day: Ford paid $5.00.

Die Hauptfertigungsstraße in Highland Park. Ford-Arbeiter gehörten zu den bestbezahlten in den Vereinigten Staaten. Damals betrug der nationale Durchschnittslohn 2,40 Dollar am Tag; Ford zahlte 5 Dollar.

Ensemble de la chaîne de montage à Highland Park. Les salaires des ouvriers de Ford figuraient parmi les plus élevés des États-Unis. À cette époque, le salaire national moyen était de 2,40 $ par jour, celui de Ford était de 5,00 $.

Claude Grahame-White, one of the greatest British aviation pioneers, takes off in a Farman III biplane from outside the White House on Executive Avenue, Washington DC, 4 October 1910.

Claude Grahame-White, einer der größten britischen Flugpioniere, hebt in einem Farman-III-Doppeldecker von der Executive Avenue vor dem Weißen Haus ab, Washington, D. C., 4. Oktober 1910.

Claude Grahame-White, un des plus grands pionniers de l'aviation britannique, décolle à bord d'un biplan Farman III à l'extérieur de la Maison-Blanche sur Executive Avenue à Washington DC, le 4 octobre 1910.

A Bristol Prier monoplane from the Bristol Flying School circles over Stonehenge, Wiltshire, in 1911. Notable landmarks such as Stonehenge were invaluable navigation aids for early pilots.

Ein Bristol-Prier-Eindecker der Flugschule von Bristol kreist über Stonehenge, Wiltshire, 1911. Auffällige Landmarken wie Stonehenge waren eine unschätzbare Navigationshilfe für die frühen Piloten.

Un monoplan Bristol Pier appartenant à l'école de pilotage de Bristol survole Stonehenge (Wiltshire), en 1911. Des points de repère aussi reconnaissables que le site de Stonehenge étaient d'un grand secours pour les pilotes de cette époque.

Stunt flyer Lincoln
Beachey in a Curtiss
biplane races against
Barney Oldfield in
his Christie, Ascot
Park, Los Angeles,
14 February 1914.

Der Kunstflieger
Lincoln Beachey,
in einem Curtiss-
Doppeldecker,
fliegt ein Rennen
gegen Barney
Oldfield in seinem
Christie, Ascot Park,
Los Angeles,
14. Februar 1914.

Le pilote cascadeur
Lincoln Beachey
à bord d'un biplan
Curtiss fait la course
avec Barney Oldfield
au volant d'une
Christie, à Ascot
Park (Los Angeles),
le 14 février 1914.

The west crossover junction of the District, Circle and Whitechapel lines, a short distance from Liverpool Street Underground station, 30 July 1912. From 1914, London's transport system was ruled by Albert Stanley, later Lord Ashfield.

Der westliche Kreuzungspunkt der District-, Circle- und Whitechapel-Linien unweit des U-Bahnhofes Liverpool Street, 30. Juli 1912. Von 1914 an wurde das Londoner Verkehrssystem von Albert Stanley, später Lord Ashfield, geleitet.

Voies de croisement à l'embranchement ouest des lignes District, Circle et Whitechapel, non loin de la station de métro Liverpool Street, le 30 juillet 1912. À partir de 1914, le réseau de transport londonien fut dirigé par Albert Stanley, futur Lord Ashfield.

A down-to-earth lesson in flying for Princess Ludwig of Löwenstein-Wertheim, 12 June 1914. Sharing the dual controls with Her Highness is Mr Baumann of the Beatty Flying School.

Eine Bodenübung im Fliegen für Prinzessin Ludwig von Löwenstein-Wertheim, 12. Juni 1914. Neben Ihrer Hoheit sitzt am zweiten Steuerrad Mr. Baumann von der Beatty Flying School.

Une leçon de pilotage très terre-à-terre pour la princesse Ludwig de Löwenstein-Wertheim, le 12 juin 1914. Monsieur Baumann de l'école d'aviation de Beatty a le grand honneur de partager les commandes avec son Altesse.

The soaring imagination of designers in the early days of flying produced many strange-looking craft – few of which actually managed to soar. One such was the Roshon multiplane (above) of 1910.

Die hochfliegenden Pläne der Designer in der Frühzeit des Flugzeugs brachten mancherlei merkwürdig anmutende Gefährte hervor – die wenigsten davon flogen allerdings auch selbst hoch. Dazu gehörte auch der Roshon-Vielfachdecker von 1910.

L'imagination débordante des premiers concepteurs d'avion produisit d'étranges engins. Rares étaient ceux qui parvenaient à s'élever dans les airs, comme ce multi-plan Roshon (ci-dessus) de 1910.

GANTRY SIGNALS, RUGBY.

A gantry of forty-four signals at Rugby, on the London and North West Railway. Rugby was a 'railway town' on the main line from London to the north of England and Scotland.

Eine Signalbrücke mit 44 Signalen bei Rugby auf der Strecke der London and North West Railway. Rugby war eine „Eisenbahnerstadt" an der Hauptstrecke von London in den Norden Englands und nach Schottland.

Portique équipé de 44 signaux à Rugby sur la ligne de Londres et du Nord-Ouest. Rugby était une « ville de voies ferrées » établie sur la ligne principale allant de Londres au nord de l'Angleterre et en Écosse.

13. Sport
Sport
Le sport

George Burdett thwarts a Liverpool attack on the Woolwich Arsenal goal,
2 September 1911. Three years later, the club dropped 'Woolwich' and
became simply 'Arsenal'.

George Burdett im Tor von Woolwich Arsenal macht am 2. September 1911
einen Angriff von Liverpool zunichte. Drei Jahre später ließ der Club das
„Woolwich" fallen und hieß fortan einfach „Arsenal".

George Burdett déjoue une attaque de Liverpool qui tente de marquer
contre Woolwich Arsenal, le 2 septembre 1911. Trois ans plus tard, le club
supprimait «Woolwich» pour devenir «Arsenal», tout simplement.

13. Sport
Sport
Le sport

The era of amateur supremacy in sport was drawing to an end. Professionals carried all before them in every sport save those most jealously guarded by the gentleman player. In 1913 Jim Thorpe was stripped of the gold medals he had won in the Stockholm Olympics, when it was discovered that he had once played minor league baseball as a professional. England still managed to defeat most countries in the sports that the British had exported to the rest of the world, but her supremacy was being challenged by the Australians (cricket), the Americans (tennis, boxing and golf) and the Scots (football).

Sport was still divided into the muddy trials of strength of the working classes and the subtle contests of skill favoured by the well-to-do. Thousands stood on windswept, rain-lashed terraces roaring on their football heroes. Hundreds raised their parasols in appreciation of a telling shot on the croquet lawn. Money tended to decide which to favour.

And already there were instances of violence in sport. In May 1912 baseball star Ty Cobb was banned from playing after he climbed into a stand to pummel an abusive spectator. The 20th century had truly arrived.

Die Ära, in der Amateure den Sport dominierten, stand kurz vor dem Ende. Die Professionellen gaben überall den Ton an, außer in den Bereichen, die von den „Gentleman"-Sportlern eifersüchtig bewacht wurden. Im Jahre 1913 wurden Jim Thorpe die Goldmedaillen aberkannt, die er bei den Olympischen Spielen von Stockholm gewonnen hatte, als herauskam, dass er einmal als Berufssportler in einer unteren Liga Baseball gespielt hatte. England gelang es immer noch, die meisten Länder in den Sportarten zu besiegen, die die Briten in die übrige Welt exportiert hatten, aber diese Vormachtstellung wurde von den Australiern (im Kricket), den Amerikanern (im Tennis, Boxen und Golf) und den Schotten (im Fußball) angegriffen.

Der Sport war noch immer gespalten in die Schlammschlachten des Kräftemessens der Arbeiterklasse und den edlen Wettstreit technischen Könnens, der von den Wohlhabenden favorisiert wurde. Tausende standen auf windigen, von Regengüssen gepeitschten Rängen und feuerten brüllend ihre Fußballhelden an. Hunderte hoben und senkten die Sonnenschirme als Beifall für einen gelungenen Schlag auf dem Krocketrasen. Geld entschied darüber, was bevorzugt wurde.

Und es gab auch schon Beispiele von Gewalttätigkeit im Sport. Im Mai 1912 wurde der Baseballstar Ty Cobb gesperrt, nachdem er auf die Tribüne geklettert war und sich bei einem Zuschauer für Beleidigungen mit Schlägen revanchiert hatte. Jetzt hatte das 20. Jahrhundert wirklich angefangen.

L'ère de la suprématie du sport amateur touchait à sa fin. Les professionnels faisaient leurs chemins dans tous les sports, excepté dans certaines sphères protégées et réservées aux gens de la haute société. En 1913, Jim Thorpe fut dépouillé de ses médailles d'or gagnées aux Jeux olympiques de Stockholm pour avoir jadis joué comme professionnel dans une petite équipe de base-ball. L'Angleterre réussissait encore à vaincre la quasi-totalité des pays vers lesquels les Britanniques avaient exporté leurs sports, mais cette suprématie serait bientôt remise en cause par les Australiens (cricket), les Américains (tennis, boxe et golf) et les Écossais (football).

Le sport était encore divisé en deux camps, avec les combats de force boueux pour les ouvriers et les subtils tournois d'adresse pour les riches. Pendant que des milliers de gens se pressaient aux abords d'un terrain exposé au vent et à la pluie et hurlaient des encouragements à leurs héros de football, des centaines de personnes se réunissaient sur une pelouse de croquet et élevaient leurs ombrelles chaque fois qu'elles appréciaient un joli coup. C'était souvent l'argent qui décidait du sport que l'on pratiquerait.

À cette époque déjà, des incidents violents entachaient le sport. En mai 1912, la star du base-ball Ty Cobb fut suspendu pour avoir grimpé dans une tribune et rué de coups un spectateur qui avait été injurieux. Le XXe siècle avait réellement commencé.

Jim Thorpe wins
the discus stage of
the Pentathlon,
Stockholm, June
1912. His throw set
a new world record.

Jim Thorpe gewinnt
den Diskuswurf
im Fünfkampf,
Stockholm,
Juni 1912. Sein
Wurf war neuer
Weltrekord.

Jim Thorpe
remporte l'épreuve
du disque au
pentathlon de
Stockholm, juin
1912. Son lancer
établit un nouveau
record mondial.

Mr Bryce enjoys a round of golf, 1910. The British Open was dominated in the 1910s by James Braid and Harry Vardon.

Mr. Bryce genießt eine Runde Golf, 1910. Die British Open wurde in diesem Jahrzehnt von James Braid und Harry Vardon dominiert.

M. Bryce goûte au plaisir d'une partie de golf, 1910. L'Open britannique des années 1910 fut dominé par James Braid et Harry Vardon.

Jack Johnson,
World Heavyweight
Champion,
2 February 1914.
Johnson had already
fled from the States
and was living
in Europe.

Jack Johnson,
Weltmeister im
Schwergewicht, am
2. Februar 1914.
Johnson war damals
schon aus den Staa-
ten geflohen und
lebte in Europa.

Jack Johnson,
champion du monde
des poids lourds, le
2 février 1914.
Johnson avait déjà
fui les États-Unis et
vivait en Europe.

Walter Mead, the
'Essex Treasure',
near the end of his
cricketing career,
1910. Mead was
a slow-medium
bowler of
impeccable length.

Walter Mead, der
„Essex Treasure"
(„Schatz von
Essex"), kurz vor
Ende seiner Kricket-
karriere, 1910.
Mead war ein lang-
samer bis mittlerer
Werfer mit einem
untrüglichen Gespür
für Weite.

Walter Mead, la
« perle de l'Essex »,
vers la fin de sa
carrière de cricket,
1910. Mead fut
un lanceur « slow-
medium » à la
portée admirable.

Taking a punt – Oldham Athletic v Tottenham Hotspur, 11 December 1911.
It was the first season in which goalkeepers were allowed to handle the ball in
the penalty area only.

Abschlag – Oldham Athletic gegen Tottenham Hotspur, 11. Dezember 1911.
Es war die erste Saison, in der Torhüter den Ball nur noch im Strafraum mit
der Hand berühren durften.

Dégagement du ballon – Oldham Athletic contre Tottenham Hotspur, le
11 décembre 1911. Ce fut la première saison au cours de laquelle les gardiens
de but furent autorisés à toucher le ballon dans l'aire de penalty uniquement.

Taking the plunge.
One of the
competitors in
the diving events
at the Stockholm
Olympics, 1912.

Absprung. Einer der
Mitbewerber im
Turmspringen bei
den Olympischen
Spielen in Stock-
holm, 1912.

Piquer un plongeon.
Un des concurrents
de l'épreuve de
plongeon lors des
Jeux olympiques de
Stockholm, 1912.

(Above and opposite) A brace of low bounces at the Queen's Club, Hurlingham, London. (Above) Miss May Turner hurries forward, August 1918. The club was a centre for polo, skittles, croquet, swimming, golf and pigeon shooting, as well as tennis.

(Oben und gegenüberliegende Seite) Zwei tief platzierte Schläge im Queen's Club, Hurlingham, London. (Oben) Miss May Turner eilt dem Ball entgegen, August 1918. Außer für Tennis war der Club auch ein Zentrum für Polo, Kegeln, Krocket, Schwimmen, Golf und Taubenschießen.

(Ci-dessus et ci-contre) Échanges de coups bien bas au Queen's Club de Hurlingham à Londres. (Ci-dessus) Mlle May Turner s'avance en courant vers la balle, août 1918. Le club était un centre sportif incluant le polo, les quilles, le croquet, la natation, le golf, le tir de pigeon et le tennis.

Captain de Tessier at full stretch, the Queen's Club, June 1918.
The absence of spectators suggests that this was simply a practice
match while the captain was on leave from the Front.

Captain de Tessier in voller Streckung, im Queen's Club, Juni 1918.
Die Abwesenheit von Zuschauern legt nahe, dass es sich lediglich
um ein Übungsspiel handelte, als der Captain Fronturlaub hatte.

Le capitaine de Tessier dans toute sa longueur au Queen's Club,
juin 1918. L'absence de spectateurs laisse penser qu'il s'agit d'un
match d'entraînement au cours d'une permission, loin du front.

Two scenes from the Military Athletic Sports Meeting at Merton Park, London, August 1918. (Above) Members of the Women's Auxiliary Army Corps compete in an egg and spoon race.

Zwei Szenen vom Militärsportfest im Merton Park, London, August 1918. (Oben) Mitglieder des Frauenhilfskorps der Armee treten im Eierlaufen gegeneinander an.

Deux scènes saisies lors d'un tournoi de sports réservé aux sportifs de l'armée à Merton Park, Londres, en août 1918. (Ci-dessus) Des membres du corps des femmes auxiliaires de l'armée sont engagées dans une course d'œuf à la cuillère.

A time out of war for a tug o' war, Merton Park, August 1918.
Until its demolition in 1840, the park was the site of Merton
Place, the only house that Admiral Horatio Nelson ever owned.

Tauziehen, diesmal nicht an der Front, Merton Park, August 1918.
Bis zu seinem Abriss 1840 stand dort Merton Place, das einzige
Haus, das Admiral Horatio Nelson jemals besaß.

Tir à la corde et non pas sur l'ennemi, Merton Park, août 1918.
Merton Place, la seule demeure que posséda jamais l'amiral
Horatio Nelson et qui fut détruite en 1840, avait été élevée
dans ce parc.

A string of thoroughbreds sets out for early morning training on
English downland, 1910. In the last year of the reign of Edward VII,
horse racing was very much the Sport of Kings.

Eine Kette von Vollblutpferden macht sich auf den Weg zum
frühmorgendlichen Training in den Niederungen Englands, 1910.
Im letzten Regierungsjahr von Edward VII. war Pferderennen der
Sport der Könige.

Une lignée de pur-sang en route pour un entraînement matinal dans
les basses terres anglaises, 1910. Durant la dernière année du règne
du roi Édouard VII, la course de chevaux devint un sport de roi.

A section of the crowd at the FA Cup Final, Crystal Palace, April 1914. It was the first attended by royalty, though George V had a seat to himself. Burnley beat Liverpool 1-0.

Ein Teil der Zuschauer beim englischen Pokalfinale, Crystal Palace, April 1914, dem ersten unter königlichen Augen. Allerdings hatte George V. einen eigenen Sitzplatz. Burnley schlug Liverpool 1:0.

Une partie du public durant la finale de la coupe d'Angleterre au Crystal Palace, avril 1914. Ce fut le premier match auquel assista un monarque et, bien sûr, Georges V occupa un siège réservé à son attention. Burnley battit Liverpool 1 à 0.

Up and over. Horse and rider in precipitous flight at a steeplechase meeting in Ireland, 1910. Injuries to both were more frequent in the early part of the 20th century than today.

Auf und darüber. Pferd und Reiter im verhängnisvollen Flug bei einem Jagdrennen in Irland, 1910. Beide wurden zu Beginn des 20. Jahrhunderts häufiger verletzt als heute.

Saut et chute. Le cheval et son cavalier pris dans un envol précipité lors d'un steeple-chase en Irlande, 1910. Il était plus fréquent de voir les deux blessés au début du XXe siècle qu'aujourd'hui.

Up and away. W L Brock, at the controls of a Blériot monoplane, avoids the central pylon at the Hendon Air Show, London, 15 November 1913. Pilots in the early days of aviation were bold rather than conscientious spirits.

Auf und davon. W. L. Brock, am Steuer eines Blériot-Eindeckers, weicht bei der Hendon-Flugschau in London am 15. November 1913 knapp dem Signalmast aus. In den Kindertagen der Luftfahrt waren Piloten eher tollkühn als umsichtig.

Envol et chute ? W. L. Brock, aux manettes de son monoplan Blériot, évite le pylône central lors du show aérien de Hendon à Londres, le 15 novembre 1913. Les pilotes des débuts de l'aviation étaient plus audacieux que consciencieux.

Johnny Marquis
turns his Sunbeam
over at Death Curve
during the 35th
lap of the Santa
Monica Grand
Prix, California,
16 March 1914.
Both Marquis
and his mechanic
survived.

Johnny Marquis legt
am 16. März 1914
in der 35. Runde
des Santa Monica
Grand Prix, Kali-
fornien, seinen
Sunbeam in der so
genannten Todes-
kurve aufs Kreuz.
Marquis und sein
Mechaniker über-
lebten den Unfall.

La Sunbeam de
Johnny Marquis se
renverse dans le
« virage mòrtel »
au 35ᵉ tour du
Grand Prix de Santa
Monica (Californie),
le 16 mars 1914.
Marquis et son
mécanicien survé-
curent à l'accident.

14. Children
Kinder
Les enfants

Bath-time for a larger than average family in a richer than average household, August 1919. This bathroom is a far cry from the old-fashioned tin bath in front of the kitchen fire.

Badezeit bei einer überdurchschnittlich großen Familie in einem überdurchschnittlich reichen Haushalt, August 1919. Dieses Badezimmer ist meilenweit entfernt von der altmodischen Zinkwanne vor dem Küchenherd.

C'est l'heure du bain pour les enfants d'une famille plus grande que la moyenne vivant dans une maison plus confortable que la moyenne, août 1919. Cette baignoire diffère totalement de l'ancienne bassine en fer que l'on installait devant la cheminée de la cuisine.

14. Children
Kinder
Les enfants

Life for children was improving. New ideas were trickling into the education systems of the West. Doctor Maria Montessori opened schools for the very young based on the principles of spontaneity of expression and freedom from restraint. The sisters McMillan established clinics that revolutionised health care for slum children. Societies for the prevention of cruelty to children were founded in the USA and many European countries.

The school curriculum was based on literacy and numeracy, with a great deal of religious instruction, and a smattering of geography and a foreign language. Both before and during the First World War, history teaching was little more than a jingristic catalogue of glorious achievements. In 1911 a group of English schoolchildren organised a strike against corporal punishment. They were lured back to school with promises of no recrimination. The promises were not kept. Diet did, however, improve. Dehydrated milk replaced the sugar and cornflour that had contributed to the high levels of infant mortality. At the same time, the birth rate declined. Whereas the average family held six children fifty years earlier, by 1910 most parents stopped at two. Life was better, but it was not yet good enough.

Das Leben der Kinder verbesserte sich. In die Bildungssysteme des Westens flossen nach und nach neue Ideen ein. Dr. Maria Montessori eröffnete Schulen für die Jüngsten, deren Grundsätze Spontaneität des Ausdrucks und Freiheit von Restriktionen waren. Die McMillan-Schwestern richteten Krankenhäuser ein, die die Gesundheitsfürsorge für Kinder in Elendsvierteln revolutionierten. Gesellschaften zur Verhinderung von Grausamkeit gegen Kinder wurden in den USA und in vielen Ländern Europas gegründet.

Die Hauptpfeiler der schulischen Lehrpläne waren die elementaren Fähigkeiten Lesen, Schreiben und Rechnen, dazu kamen ein gehöriger Anteil Religionsunterricht und ein paar

Brocken Erdkunde und Fremdsprachen. Vor und während des Ersten Weltkrieges bestand Geschichtsunterricht aus wenig mehr als einem Katalog der patriotischen Errungenschaften. Im Jahr 1911 organisierte eine Gruppe englischer Schulkinder einen Streik gegen körperliche Züchtigung. Die Kinder wurden mit dem Versprechen der Straffreiheit in die Schule zurückgelockt, aber das Versprechen wurde gebrochen. Die Ernährung wurde besser. Milchpulver konnte Zucker und Stärkemehl ersetzen, die zu einer hohen Kindersterblichkeit beigetragen hatten. Gleichzeitig sank die Geburtenrate. Während 50 Jahre zuvor eine Durchschnittsfamilie noch sechs Kinder gehabt hatte, begnügten sich 1910 die meisten Eltern mit zwei Kindern. Das Leben war besser, aber es war noch nicht gut genug.

La vie des enfants s'améliorait. Petit à petit, de nouvelles théories parvenaient à s'imposer dans les systèmes éducatifs occidentaux. Le Dr. Maria Montessori ouvrit des écoles pour les jeunes enfants dont les principes reposaient sur la libre expression et l'absence de contraintes. Le sœurs McMillan mirent en place des dispensaires qui révolutionnèrent les soins médicaux donnés aux enfants des quartiers pauvres. Des associations de prévention contre la maltraitance infantile furent fondées aux États-Unis et dans de nombreux pays européens.

Les programmes scolaires furent élaborés autour de l'apprentissage de l'écriture, de la lecture et du calcul, une grande place étant réservée à l'instruction religieuse et une toute petite à la géographie et aux langues étrangères. Quant à l'enseignement de l'histoire, que ce soit avant ou durant la Première Guerre mondiale, il se résumait à un inventaire des glorieuses réussites de la mère patrie. En 1911, un groupe d'écoliers anglais se mit en grève pour protester contre le châtiment corporel. Ils reprirent le chemin de l'école après qu'on leur eut promis qu'il n'y aurait pas de sanction, mais ces promesses ne furent pas tenues. L'alimentation s'améliora. Le lait déshydraté remplaça le sucre et la farine de maïs qui avaient contribué à maintenir un taux de mortalité infantile élevé. Parallèlement, le taux de natalité déclinait. Cinquante ans plus tôt, chaque famille comptait six enfants en moyenne, mais en 1910 la plupart des parents s'arrêtaient au deuxième enfant. La vie était meilleure, mais elle n'était pas encore assez bonne.

This may well be the same happy family depicted in the chapter opener.
The date and the composition of the family are the same. The Decca
wind-up gramophone denotes considerable affluence.

Dies kann durchaus die glückliche Familie sein, die auf dem Eingangsfoto
zu diesem Kapitel abgebildet ist. Das Datum und die Anzahl der Kinder
entsprechen sich. Das Decca-Grammophon mit Aufziehmechanismus
spricht für erheblichen Wohlstand.

Il est probable que cette famille soit la même que celle qui figure en
ouverture de ce chapitre. La date et le nombre d'enfants sont identiques.
Le gramophone Decca est la preuve qu'il s'agit d'un milieu très aisé.

Pupils of Miss Morris's Academy, London, October 1912. Noël Coward recalled
happy hours at such an establishment: 'I loved my dancing lessons… the whole
routine of ballet dancing, for which I wore block-toed shoes…'

Schülerinnen von Miss Morris's Academy, London, Oktober 1912. Noël Coward
erinnerte sich später an glückliche Stunden in einer solchen Einrichtung: „Ich liebte
meine Tanzstunden sehr … die ganze Routine des Balletts, für das ich richtige
Ballettschuhe trug …"

Élèves de l'école de Miss Morris, Londres, octobre 1912. Noël Coward n'a pas oublié
les joyeux moments passés dans ce genre d'établissement : « J'adorais mes leçons de
danse … et toute la routine du ballet, pour lequel je chaussais mes pointes … »

The interior of an East End tenement, London, July 1912. Public housing and private philanthropy – such as the Peabody Housing Estates – were gradually replacing the worst of the slums, but there was much still to do.

Eine Wohnung im Londoner East End, Juli 1912. Sozialer Wohnungsbau und private Wohltätigkeitsinitiativen – wie die Peabody Housing Estates – ersetzten nach und nach die schlimmsten Elendsquartiere, aber es gab noch viel zu tun.

Intérieur d'un logement dans l'East End à Londres, juillet 1912. Les logements des services sociaux et des associations philanthropiques privées, comme les cités Peabody, remplacèrent progressivement les taudis les plus misérables, mais il y avait encore beaucoup à faire.

A young rat-catcher checks her night's haul in the backyard, May 1916. Rats were commonplace residents of most houses in the early 20th century, and did not provoke the degree of horror that they do now.

Eine junge Rattenfängerin überprüft im Mai 1916 im Hinterhof ihren Fang. Ratten waren im frühen 20. Jahrhundert ganz normale Mitbewohner vieler Häuser und erregten nicht so viel Abscheu wie heute.

Une jeune chasseuse de rats fait l'inventaire de sa prise nocturne dans une arrière-cour, mai 1916. Les rats étaient des habitants ordinaires de la plupart des maisons du début du XXᵉ siècle et ne suscitaient pas autant d'horreur qu'aujourd'hui.

The wheels of fortune. (Above) Children take to the street in a well-made go-kart. (Opposite) Soldiers stand guard over two young children during the civil disturbances in Berlin, December 1914.

Die Glücksräder. Kinder erobern die Straße in einer gut gebauten Seifenkiste. (Gegenüberliegende Seite) Soldaten wachen während Bürgerunruhen in Berlin über zwei kleine Kinder, Dezember 1914.

Les roues de la fortune. (Ci-dessus) Des enfants s'amusent dans la rue avec une voiture bien conçue. (Ci-contre) Des soldats en poste gardent ces deux jeunes enfants durant les troubles à Berlin, 1914.

Wartime protest. A children's march in support of Prohibition, west London, 23 June 1917. The banner reads: 'We growing children must have bread & sugar.' Drink was seen as a cause of poverty.

Protest zu Kriegszeiten. Kinder marschieren für die Prohibition, Westlondon, 23. Juni 1917. Auf dem Plakat steht: „Wir Kinder wachsen und brauchen Brot und Zucker". Die Trunksucht wurde als Ursache für Armut angesehen.

Revendications pendant la guerre. Une manifestation d'enfants en faveur de la prohibition, quartier ouest de Londres, le 23 juin 1917. La pancarte dit : « Les enfants qui grandissent ont besoin de pain et de sucre ». L'alcool était considéré comme une cause de pauvreté.

Peacetime charity. Children queue for soup at the Canterbury Music Hall, Kent. Most poor children were raised on tinned beef and tinned milk. The absence of fruit and vegetables in their diet led to world-wide outbreaks of scurvy.

Wohltätigkeit in Friedenszeiten. Kinder stellen sich in der Canterbury Music Hall in Kent für Suppe an. Die Kinder der Armen wurden mit Dosenrindfleisch und Dosenmilch hochgepäppelt. Der Mangel an Obst und Gemüse in ihrer Ernährung führte weltweit zu Ausbrüchen von Skorbut.

Charité en temps de paix. Des enfants font la queue au music-hall de Canterbury (Kent). La majorité des enfants défavorisés étaient nourris avec du bœuf en boîte et du lait concentré. L'absence de fruits et de légumes dans leur alimentation engendra des épidémies de scorbut partout dans le monde.

Flowers for the dead. Schoolgirls pay their respects to an air-raid victim, Folkestone, 29 May 1917. Though there were few such casualties in the First World War, the shock of death from the skies horrified civilians.

Blumen für die Toten. Schulmädchen erweisen dem Opfer eines Luftangriffs die letzte Ehre, Folkestone, 29. Mai 1917. Obwohl es im Ersten Weltkrieg wenige solcher Opfer gab, verschreckte der plötzliche Tod aus den Wolken die Zivilbevölkerung zutiefst.

Fleurs pour un défunt. Des écolières rendent hommage à la victime d'un raid aérien, le 29 mai 1917. Bien qu'il y ait eu peu de victimes de ces raids durant la Première Guerre mondiale, les civils étaient horrifiés par la brutalité de cette mort venue du ciel.

Work for the living. A young boy helps his father deliver coal, August 1919. The widespread laws limiting child labour had not yet been rigorously enforced.

Arbeit für die Lebenden. Ein kleiner Junge hilft seinem Vater beim Ausliefern von Kohle, August 1919. Die zahlreichen Gesetze zur Begrenzung von Kinderarbeit wurden noch nicht streng durchgesetzt.

Travail pour les vivants. Un petit garçon aide son père, livreur de charbon, août 1919. Les nombreuses lois visant à réduire le travail des enfants n'étaient pas encore appliquées avec rigueur.

Schoolchildren contribute to the Disaster Fund in aid of the families of victims from the *Titanic* tragedy, May 1912. More than 1,500 people were drowned when the liner sank on her maiden voyage.

Schulkinder spenden für den Katastrophenfonds, der für die Angehörigen der Opfer der *Titanic*-Tragödie eingerichtet worden war, Mai 1912. Mehr als 1500 Menschen ertranken, als der Passagierdampfer auf seiner Jungfernfahrt sank.

Des enfants contribuent au fonds d'aide créé en faveur des familles des victimes de la tragédie du *Titanic*, mai 1912. Plus de 1500 personnes périrent lors du naufrage du paquebot qui effectuait sa croisière inaugurale.

A young girl posts
a letter in one of the
first pillar boxes
to be erected with
the initials of
King George V,
26 January 1911.

Ein kleines Mädchen
steckt einen Brief in
einen der ersten mit
den Initialen von
König George V. ver-
sehenen Briefkästen,
26. Januar 1911.

Une fillette dépose
une lettre dans une
des premières boîtes
aux lettres érigées
avec les initiales du
roi Georges V, le
26 janvier 1911.

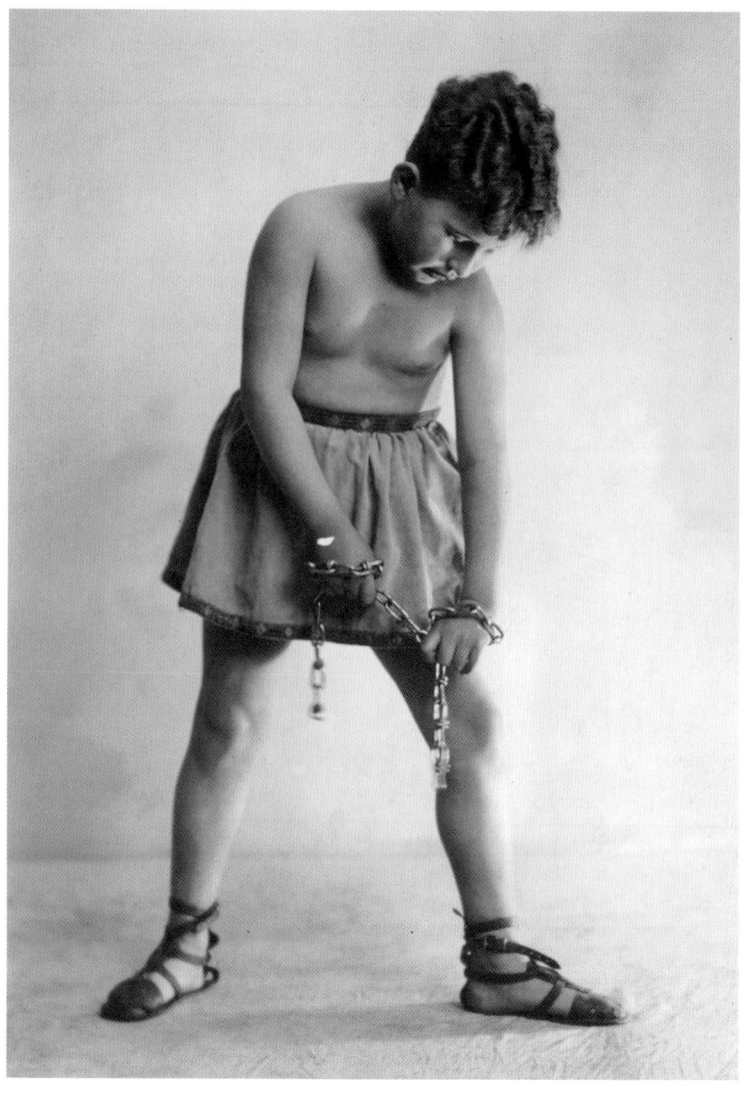

Powerful muscles. Lichterfeld, the 10-year-old strongman, prepares to break his chains.

Mächtige Muskeln. Lichterfeld, der zehnjährige Kraftprotz, schickt sich an, seine Ketten zu brechen.

Bien musclé. Lichterfeld, un hercule âgé de 10 ans, prêt à rompre ses chaînes.

Heavy frame. Nine-year-old Maurice Pluthero of Petersham, Surrey, proudly displays his 50-inch chest.

Starke Statur. Der neunjährige Maurice Pluthero aus Petersham in Surrey präsentiert stolz seinen 50-Zoll-Brustkorb (127 cm).

Bien bâti. Maurice Pluthero, âgé de 9 ans et originaire de Petersham (Surrey) affiche fièrement son buste, dont le tour fait plus d'un mètre.

A child worker in
a textile factory.
In the United States,
children as young as
six were working
thirteen-hour days,
spinning cotton.

Kinderarbeiterin in
einer Textilfabrik. In
den USA arbeiteten
schon Sechsjährige
13 Stunden am Tag
in Baumwoll-
spinnereien.

Fillette travaillant
dans l'industrie tex-
tile. Aux États-Unis,
des enfants âgés de
six ans seulement
et utilisés pour filer
le coton accomplis-
saient des journées
de treize heures.

So many to choose from, so little to spend. Children examine the delights of a doll stall in a Berlin street. Sixpence (2.5 pence) could buy a whole family of dolls imported from Japan.

So große Auswahl, so wenig auszugeben. Kinder erkunden die Freuden eines Standes mit Puppen in einer Berliner Straße. Für gut 50 Pfennige konnte man sich eine ganze Familie importierter Puppen aus Japan kaufen.

Tant de choix et si peu d'argent. Des enfants admirent un stand de poupées dans une rue de Berlin. Avec une pièce de six pence, il était possible d'acheter une famille entière de poupées importées du Japon.

An unconvincing photograph of African children playing
cricket, c. 1910. Proponents of the Empire liked to see it as
a means of bringing British culture to the rest of the world.

Eine wenig überzeugende Aufnahme von afrikanischen
Kindern beim Kricketspiel, um 1910. Befürworter des
Empire betrachteten derlei gern als Mittel zur Bereicherung
der Welt mit britischen Errungenschaften.

Ce cliché tente de faire croire que les petits Africains jouent
au cricket, vers 1910. Les défenseurs de l'Empire espéraient
par ce moyen pouvoir propager la culture britannique à
travers le monde.

Eton schoolboys set off for the College's allotments, March 1917. The 'Dig For Victory' campaign provided a welcome relief from studies and the violence of the playing fields of Eton.

Schüler des Eton College auf dem Weg zu den Schrebergärten des Internats, März 1917. Die Kampagne „Graben für den Sieg" bot eine willkommene Abwechslung vom Lernen und der Gewalt auf den Sportplätzen Etons.

Des écoliers d'Eton en route pour les jardins de l'établissement, mars 1917. La campagne intitulée « bêcher pour la victoire » offrait une alternative bienvenue aux études et à la violence qui régnait sur les terrains de jeux d'Eton.

15. All human life
Menschliches, Allzumenschliches
Les petits et les grands événements de la vie

Delighting in his own invention, Mr Lewis Sydney puts the Follyphone through its musical paces, September 1912. Amazingly, the instrument never went into mass production.

Mit sichtlicher Freude an seiner eigenen Erfindung führt Mr. Lewis Sydney das musikalische Repertoire seines Follyphone vor, September 1912. Erstaunlicherweise gelangte das Instrument nie zur Serienfertigung.

Monsieur Lewis Sydney procède à des essais sur son Follyphone, encore sous le charme de son invention, septembre 1912. Aussi étonnant que cela puisse paraître, cet instrument ne fut jamais fabriqué en série.

15. All human life
Menschliches, Allzumenschliches
Les petits et les grands événements de la vie

Strange things happened in war and peace. Sergeant James Shearer claimed he had invented a machine that could diagnose wounds and detect the approach of enemy aircraft. He was court-martialled and shot for his effrontery and wasting the time of the authorities. Nurse Cavell was shot for helping her countrymen escape the clutches of the enemy. Mata Hari was shot for espionage and indecency. Roger Casement was hanged for treason. Rasputin was poisoned, shot, stabbed, clubbed and drowned, but still seemed unwilling to die.

Scott and Amundsen raced to the South Pole. The French poet Apollinaire was arrested for stealing the *Mona Lisa*. Sarah Bernhardt lost a leg. S H Schrapp of Lawrenceburg, Indiana, cracked a joke and laughed uncontrollably for twelve hours until given an electric shock. Hugo Junkers built the first all-metal plane. Argentinians danced the tango.

There were typhoons in Japan, floods in Paris and China, earthquakes in Nicaragua, forest fires in the American Midwest, and arguments about the installation of electric advertising signs in Times Square, New York City.

Merkwürdige Dinge geschahen im Krieg und im Frieden. Sergeant James Shearer behauptete, er habe eine Maschine erfunden, mit der man Verwundungen diagnostizieren und die Annäherung feindlicher Flugzeuge entdecken könne. Er kam vor ein Kriegsgericht und wurde wegen Aufschneiderei und Verschwendung der Zeit der Behörden erschossen. Die Krankenschwester Cavell wurde erschossen, weil sie ihren Landsleuten dabei half, den Fängen des Feindes zu entkommen. Mata Hari wurde wegen Spionage und Unzucht erschossen. Roger Casement wurde wegen Verrats gehängt. Rasputin wurde vergiftet, erschossen, erdolcht, erschlagen und ertränkt und weigerte sich noch immer beharrlich zu sterben.

Scott und Amundsen lieferten sich einen Wettlauf zum Südpol. Der französische Dichter Apollinaire wurde unter der Anklage verhaftet, die Mona Lisa gestohlen zu haben. Sarah Bernhardt verlor ein Bein. S. H. Schrapp aus Lawrenceburg in Indiana machte einen Witz und musste 12 Stunden lang unkontrollierbar lachen, bis man ihm einen Stromschlag verabreichte. Hugo Junkers baute das erste Ganzmetallflugzeug. Die Argentinier tanzten den Tango.

Es gab Taifune in Japan, Überschwemmungen in Paris und China, Erdbeben in Nicaragua, Waldbrände im amerikanischen Mittelwesten und heiße Debatten darüber, ob man am Times Square in New York City elektrische Werbetafeln anbringen dürfe oder nicht.

Des choses étranges se déroulèrent durant la guerre et la paix. Le sergent James Shearer déclara avoir inventé une machine capable de déceler les maladies et de détecter l'approche d'avions ennemis. Son effronterie lui valut d'être traduit en cour martiale et exécuté pour gaspillage de temps des autorités. L'infirmière Cavell fut exécutée pour avoir aidé des compatriotes à échapper aux griffes de l'ennemi. Mata Hari fut condamnée à mort pour espionnage et indécence. Roger Casement fut pendu pour trahison. Raspoutine fut empoisonné, blessé par balle, poignardé, matraqué et coulé dans une rivière glacée, sans succomber pour autant.

Scott et Amundsen firent la course jusqu'au pôle Sud. Le poète français Apollinaire fut arrêté après avoir dérobé la Mona Lisa. Sarah Bernhardt fut amputée d'une jambe. S. H. Schrapp de Lawrenceburg dans l'Indiana (États-Unis) raconta une blague et fut pris d'un fou-rire irrésistible qui dura douze heures. Il fallut lui administrer une décharge électrique pour qu'il arrête de rire. Hugo Junkers construisit le premier avion tout en métal. Les Argentins dansaient le tango.

Il y eut des typhons au Japon, des inondations à Paris et en Chine, des tremblements de terre au Nicaragua, des incendies de forêt dans le Middle West des États-Unis et des polémiques à New York City à propos de l'installation d'enseignes électriques à Times Square.

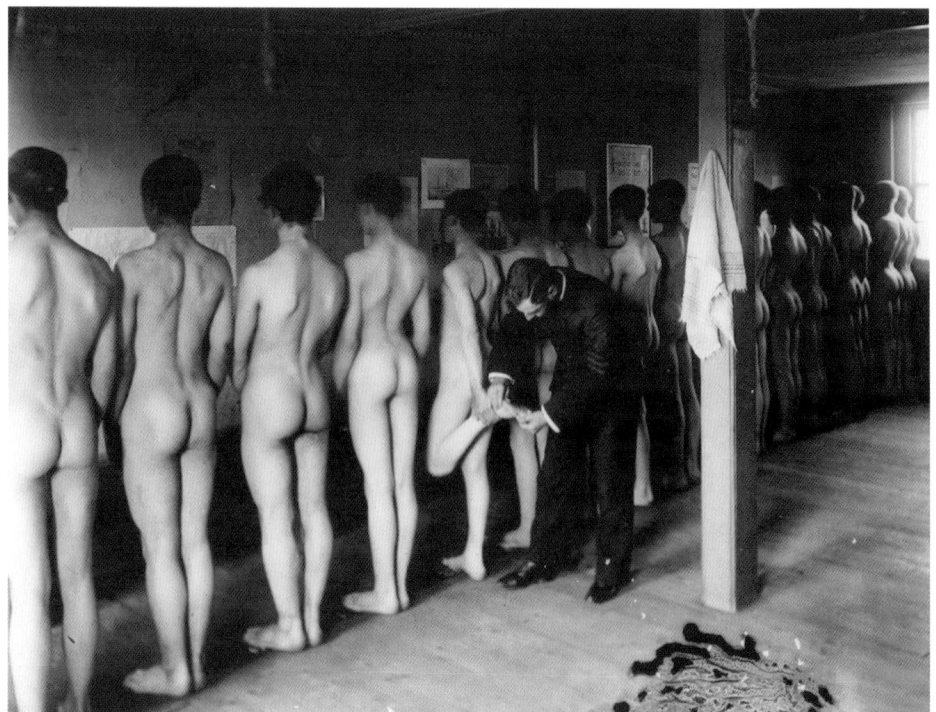

Naval recruits undergo foot examination, 1910. Few wished to kick
the enemy to death, but all branches of the services were becoming
more discerning in their selection processes.

Marinerekruten unterziehen sich einer Fußuntersuchung, 1910.
Wenige hatten vor, den Feind zu Tode zu treten, aber alle Waffen-
gattungen trafen jetzt eine sorgfältigere Auswahl.

Des recrues de la marine subissent un examen médical des pieds,
1910. Rares étaient ceux qui songeaient à envoyer un coup de pied
fatal à l'ennemi, mais les services de l'armée procédaient néanmoins
à une sélection de plus en plus détaillée des nouvelles recrues.

With remarkably little concern for their dignity, a group of men sit
with newspapers on their heads to protect themselves from the sun,
July 1913. Perhaps it did not occur to them to move into the shade.

Bemerkenswert unbekümmert um ihre Würde, schützt sich
eine Gruppe von Männern mit Zeitungen gegen die Sonne,
Juli 1913. Auf die Idee, sich in den Schatten zu setzen, kamen
sie vielleicht nicht.

Très peu soucieux de leur dignité, ces hommes sont assis avec un
journal sur la tête pour se protéger du soleil, juillet 1913. Il ne leur
était peut-être pas venu à l'esprit d'aller à l'ombre.

Separating the men from the boys and the sheep from the goats. (Left) Workmen take a crane to the top of a skyscraper, 1912. (Opposite) An animal balancing act.

Das unterscheidet Männer von Knaben und Schafe von Ziegen: (Links) Arbeiter lassen sich mit dem Kran auf einen Wolkenkratzer hieven, 1912. (Gegenüberliegende Seite) Ein tierischer Balanceakt.

Séparer les hommes des garçons et les chèvres des boucs. (Ci-dessus) Des ouvriers gagnent le sommet d'un gratte-ciel agrippés à une grue, 1912. (Ci-contre) Un numéro d'équilibre donné par des animaux.

An owner and a competitor at the twenty-first annual Cruft's
National Dog Show, London, January 1912. The show's originator,
Charles Cruft, began his professional life selling 'dog cakes'.

Mitbewerber und Besitzerin bei der 21. jährlichen Cruft's National
Dog Show, Januar 1912. Der Veranstalter der Hundeausstellung,
Charles Cruft, begann seine Karriere mit dem Verkauf von Hunde-
kuchen.

Propriétaire et concurrent participant à la 21ᵉ édition annuelle
du Salon national pour chiens, janvier 1912. Le créateur du salon,
Charles Cruft, débuta sa vie professionnelle en vendant des
« biscuits pour chien ».

Beamish's bulldog 'Beaming Blunderbus' on parade outside the twenty-first annual Belfast Dog Show, September 1912. As a symbol of Britain, the dog almost certainly had loyalist sympathies.

Beamishs Bulldogge „Beaming Blunderbus" in Positur vor der 21. jährlichen Hundeausstellung in Belfast, September 1912. Als Symbol Großbritanniens genoss der Hund sicherlich loyalistische Sympathien.

Beaming Blunderbus, le bouledogue d'un certain M. Beamish, défile à l'extérieur du 21ᵉ Salon du chien à Belfast, septembre 1912. En tant que symbole de la Grande-Bretagne, ce chien s'attirait incontestablement la sympathie des loyalistes.

(Above) Marisa (left) was 16 years old and 7 feet 4 inches tall.
Eighteen-year-old Asia was 26 inches tall. (Opposite) A couple from
the Rhine province who together weighed 1,031lb.

(Oben) Marisa (links) war 16 Jahre alt und 2 Meter 23 groß. Die
18 Jahre alte Asia war 66 cm groß. (Gegenüberliegende Seite) Ein Paar
aus dem Rheinland mit einem Gesamtgewicht von 467 kg.

(Ci-dessus) Marisa (à gauche), âgée de 16 ans, mesure 2,23 m tandis
que Asia, âgée de 18 ans, mesure 66 cm. (Ci-contre) Un couple
originaire de la région du Rhin pèse à eux deux 467 kg.

Giant Machnow and
Madame Chiquita.
The average-sized
friend was there
for reference
purposes only.

Der Riese Machnow
und Madame
Chiquita. Der
durchschnittlich
große Freund stand
nur zu Vergleichs-
zwecken daneben.

Le géant Machnow
et Madame
Chiquita, ainsi qu'un
ami dont la taille
normale facilite les
comparaisons …

Russian circus folk after the wedding of the couple in the centre, Stepney, London, 24 August 1913. There was a considerable market for displays of what were still known as 'freaks'.

Russische Zirkusleute nach der Heirat des Paares in der Mitte, Stepney, London, 24. August 1913. Es gab einen beträchtlichen Markt für Zurschaustellungen noch immer so genannter „Monstren".

Après le mariage du couple (au centre), ces membres d'un cirque russe posent pour la caméra, Stepney (Londres), le 24 août 1913. Ceux que l'on nommait encore des « monstres » étaient très demandés dans les foires.

(Opposite) Body
armour from the
First World War,
1915. (Right) Rose
Wilmot, known as
the 'ugliest woman
in London', 1919.

(Gegenüberliegende
Seite) Körperrüstung
aus dem Ersten Welt-
krieg, 1915. (Rechts)
Rose Wilmot, die
man als „hässlichste
Frau Londons"
kannte, 1919.

(Ci-contre) Armure
corporelle datant de
la Première Guerre
mondiale, 1915.
(À droite) Rose
Wilmot, connue
pour être la femme
« la plus vilaine » de
Londres, 1919.

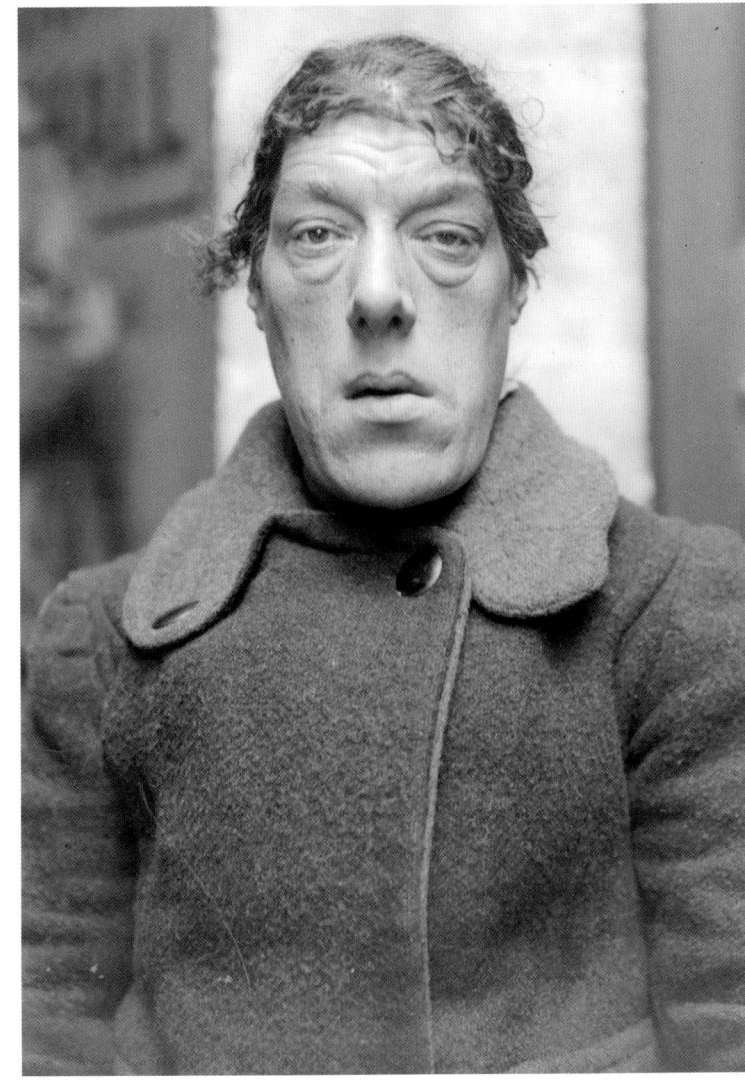

Londoners queue to read the notice posted on the railings of Buckingham Palace announcing the death of Edward VII, 6 May 1910. He had been ill for only four days, following bronchial trouble during his usual spring visit to Biarritz.

Londoner stellen sich an, um das Schild am Zaun des Buckingham Palace zu lesen, auf dem der Tod von Edward VII. bekannt gegeben wurde, 6. Mai 1910. Er war nur vier Tage lang krank gewesen, nachdem er bei seinem üblichen Frühjahrsbesuch in Biarritz Bronchialbeschwerden bekommen hatte.

Des Londoniens font la queue pour lire l'avis affiché sur les grilles du Palais de Buckingham annonçant la mort d'Édouard VII, le 6 mai 1910. Il était malade depuis quatre jours seulement, souffrant d'une bronchite attrapée lors de son rituel séjour à Biarritz au printemps.

Peers and peeresses rest their weary limbs after the Coronation of George V, 11 June 1911. The King himself recorded in his diary: 'The service in the Abbey was most beautiful, but it was a terrible ordeal…'

Peers und Peeresses verschnaufen ein wenig nach der Krönung von George V., 11. Juni 1911. Der König selbst trug in sein Tagebuch ein: „Der Gottesdienst in der Abbey war wirklich wunderschön, aber eine schreckliche Tortur …"

Pair et pairesses reposent leurs corps fatigués après le Couronnement de Georges V, le 11 juin 1911. Le roi en personne inscrivit dans son journal : « La cérémonie qui se déroula à l'Abbaye fut magnifique mais quelle terrible épreuve … ».

King George V (nearest camera, on left) exchanges his crown for
a pith helmet while picnicking with members of the royal party.
The King Emperor was in India for the Grand Durbar of 1911.

König George V. (links, am nächsten zur Kamera) tauscht beim Picknick
mit Mitgliedern des königlichen Gefolges die Krone gegen einen
Tropenhelm. Der Herrscher des Empire weilte zum Grand Durbar
(Galacour, Staatsaudienz des indischen Vizekönigs) von 1911 in Indien.

Le roi Georges V (le premier, à gauche) a échangé sa couronne pour
un casque colonial lors d'un pique-nique avec des membres de la suite
royale. Le Roi empereur était en Inde pour participer au Grand Durbar
de 1911.

In the days when only monarchs were an endangered species. The royal bag of three tigers is proudly displayed during a shoot. George V was respectfully, though inaccurately, reckoned the 'best shot in Britain'.

Zu Zeiten, da nur Monarchen eine vom Aussterben bedrohte Art waren … Bei einer Jagd wird stolz die königliche Strecke von drei Tigern präsentiert. George V. wurde respektvoll, wenn auch nicht ganz zutreffend, für den „besten Schützen Großbritanniens" gehalten.

En ce temps-là, seuls les monarques étaient une espèce en voie de disparition. Le butin royal de trois tigres est fièrement exposé durant une partie de chasse. Georges V était respectueusement surnommé « le meilleur tireur de Grande-Bretagne », même si ce n'était pas exact.

The Ball of the Coloured Wigs at the Countess Yelisaveta Shuvalova's palace in St Petersburg, 1914. The writing was already on the wall for the Russian aristocracy, but it was perhaps hidden by the flunkeys.

Der Ball der gepuderten Perücken im Palast der Gräfin Jelisaweta Schuwalowa in St. Petersburg, 1914. Für die russische Aristokratie stand die Flammenschrift bereits an der Wand, aber vielleicht wurde sie von den Lakaien verdeckt.

Bal des perruques teintées au palais de la comtesse Yelisaveta Shuvalova à Saint-Pétersbourg, 1914. L'arrêt de mort de l'aristocratie russe avait déjà été proclamé, mais cette rangée de laquais debout au fond de la salle semble cacher une telle réalité.

The interior of a slum dwelling, December 1912. Although poorly and sparsely furnished, the room appears considerably better than the worst of Britain's slums in the 1910s.

Innenansicht einer Armenwohnung, Dezember 1912. Wenn auch karg und schlicht möbliert, so wirkt der Raum doch um einiges besser als die schlimmsten der britischen Elendsviertel in diesem Jahrzehnt.

Intérieur d'une habitation d'un quartier pauvre, décembre 1912. La pièce est meublée de manière rudimentaire, mais elle semble en bien meilleur état que n'importe quel logement d'un quartier défavorisé de Grande-Bretagne dans les années 1910.

Up in flames. A balloon catches fire at an army camp in the United States, 1912. Such explosions threatened the military and commercial success of balloons and airships throughout the thirty years of their existence.

In Flammen. Ein Ballon fängt auf einem Armeestützpunkt in den USA Feuer, 1912. Derartige Explosionen bedrohten den militärischen und kommerziellen Erfolg von Ballonen und Luftschiffen während der gesamten 30 Jahre ihrer Existenz.

Ciel en feu. Un ballon s'enflamme sur une base militaire, États-Unis, 1912. De telles explosions compromettaient à chaque fois le succès militaire et commercial des ballons et dirigeables tout au long de leurs trente ans d'existence.

Down in smoke.
The collapse of an
ancient Portuguese
campanile.

Zusammenbruch in
einer Staubwolke.
Ein alter portugiesi-
scher Glockenturm
stürzt ein.

Terre enfumée.
Effondrement d'un
vieux campanile
portugais.

The music goes
round and round…
A French horn
player from a brass
band gives his all.

Und die Musik geht
immer weiter …
Ein französischer
Hornist aus einer
Blaskapelle gibt
sein Bestes.

En avant la
musique …
Ce joueur de cor
français, membre
d'une fanfare, y met
tout son souffle.

...and it comes out here. Thomas Alva Edison listens to one of his own phonographs, 27 October 1911.

... und hier kommt sie heraus. Thomas Alva Edison lauscht einem seiner eigenen Phonographen, 27. Oktober 1911.

... et voilà où il ressort. Thomas Alva Edison teste d'une oreille attentive un de ses phonographes, 27 octobre 1911.

Index

gettyimages

Over 70 million images and 30,000 hours of film footage are held by the various collections owned by Getty Images. These cover a vast number of subjects from the earliest photojournalism to current press photography, sports, social history and geography. Getty Images' conceptual imagery is renowned amongst creative end users.
www.gettyimages.com

Über 70 Millionen Bilder und 30 000 Stunden Film befinden sich in den verschiedenen Archiven von Getty Images. Sie decken ein breites Spektrum an Themen ab – von den ersten Tagen des Fotojournalismus bis hin zu aktueller Pressefotografie, Sport, Sozialgeschichte und Geographie. Bei kreativen Anwendern ist das Material von Getty Images für seine ausdrucksstarke Bildsprache bekannt.
www.gettyimages.com

Plus de 70 millions d'images et 30 000 heures de films sont détenus par les différentes collections dont Getty Images est le propriétaire. Cela couvre un nombre considérable de sujets – des débuts du photojournalisme aux photographies actuelles de presse, de sport, d'histoire sociale et de géographie. Le concept photographique de Getty Images est reconnu des créatifs.
www.gettyimages.com